Laura **Clyde**   Ray

NEW Pass Trinity

Student's Book

Trinity Grades ISE I

5-6

contents

Contents

Phonology	Exam Expert Topic (T) & Conversation (C)	Writing
Have in the Present Perfect	Preparing for the Topic phase (T) Dos and don'ts (C)	Exam & portfolio practice
Intonation of basic question forms	Preparing & presenting your topic (T)	Exam & portfolio practice
Intonation of more complex question forms	Responding to the examiner (T) Exam practice (C)	Exam & portfolio practice
-ed past tense endings	Showing understanding of the examiner (C) Exam practice (C)	Exam & portfolio practice
Sentence stress to clarify meaning	Preparing questions for the interview (C)	Exam & portfolio practice
–	Exam practice (C) Topic structure (T) Dos and don'ts (T)	Exam & portfolio practice
Connected speech at sentence level	Talking about your portfolio (C)	Exam & portfolio practice
Intonation at sentence level and of more complex forms	Exam practice (C) Choosing a topic (T)	Exam & portfolio practice

exam overview

TRINITY GRADED EXAMINATIONS IN SPOKEN ENGLISH (GESE), GRADES 5 AND 6, AND INTEGRATED SKILLS IN ENGLISH (ISE), LEVEL I

GESE Grades 5 & 6 (CEFR B1)

Time: 10 minutes

Format and procedure:

1 Discussion of a **topic prepared by the candidate** (up to 5 minutes):
- Give **information about the prepared topic** and **answer questions**.
- **Ask the examiner at least one question** about the topic area.

2 Conversation on two subject areas selected by the examiner (up to 5 minutes):
- **Answer appropriately** to questions and give information **in simple and direct exchanges**.
- **Ask the examiner at least one question** (Grade 5)/**two questions** (Grade 6) about a subject area.

Grade 5 exam syllabus:

Grammar
- Present Perfect tense including use with *for*, *since*, *ever*, *never*, *just*
- connecting clauses using *because*
- *will* for informing and predicting the future
- adjectives and adverbials of quantity, e.g. *a lot (of)*, *not very much*, *many...*
- expressions of preference, e.g. *I prefer*, *I'd rather...*

Subject areas for Conversation phase
- festivals
- means of transport
- special occasions, e.g. birthday celebrations
- entertainment, e.g. cinema, television, clubs
- music
- recent personal experiences

Functions
- talking about the future (informing and predicting)
- expressing preferences
- talking about events in the indefinite and recent past
- giving reasons
- stating the duration of events
- quantifying

Phonology
- correct pronunciation of words relevant to the vocabulary for this grade
- combination of weak forms and contractions, e.g. *I've been to...*
- avoidance of speech patterns of recitation

Grade 6 exam syllabus:

Grammar

- zero and first conditionals, using *if* and *when*
- Present Continuous tense for future use
- Past Continuous tense
- modals: *must, need to, might, don't have to*
- infinitive of purpose

Subject areas for Conversation phase

- travel
- money
- fashion
- rules and regulations
- health and fitness
- learning a foreign language

Functions

- expressing and requesting opinions
- expressing intention and purpose
- expressing obligation and necessity
- expressing certainty and uncertainty
- describing past actions over a period of time

Phonology

- correct pronunciation of words relevant to the vocabulary for this grade
- sentence stress to clarify meaning
- intonation patterns of more complex question forms

ISE I

Portfolio Tasks

Format:

- **Candidates must complete one task from each section** (see below) during class time or individual study. The tasks must be selected from the list for the current year found on the Trinity College website.

Section 1 (70-80 words)
correspondence task
e.g. letter, email

Section 2 (110-130 words)
factual writing task
e.g. report, article, review

Section 3 (110-130 words)
creative/descriptive task
e.g. diary, story, description

Controlled Written examination

Time: 1 hour 30 minutes
Format:

- Candidates must complete both tasks on this exam paper. No choice of tasks is given.

Task 1
Reading into Writing (150 words): you read a text and then complete a task based on information from the text

Task 2
Writing task (150 words): a similar task to those required in the portfolio but without extra support material

The interview

Time: 8 minutes
Format:

- Discussion of a **topic prepared by the candidate** (up to 4 minutes)
- Conversation with the examiner **including a discussion of the portfolio and one subject area from Grade 6 list selected by the examiner** (up to 4 minutes)

diagnostic test

Listen to the examiner asking some questions and choose the best answer, A, B or C. There is only one right answer for each question. You will hear each question only ONCE. Good luck!

1
  A My name Gianluca.
  B My name's Gianluca.
  C Is Gianluca.

2
  A I've 17.
  B I'm 17.
  C Fine, thanks. And You?

3
  A She's blue.
  B He's blue.
  C It's blue.

4
  A There are seven.
  B They are seven.
  C We have seven.

5
  A I am of Trieste.
  B I come to Trieste.
  C I come from Trieste.

6
  A Yes, I got a dog.
  B Yes, I've got a dog.
  C Yes, I have got.

7
  A Her name is Paola.
  B She name is Paola.
  C Her name Paola.

8
  A He has two.
  B He is two.
  C He two.

9
  A It's opposite of the supermarket.
  B It opposite the supermarket.
  C It's opposite the supermarket.

10
  A It's today.
  B It's Monday.
  C Is Monday.

11
  A I live in Madrid.
  B I live at Madrid.
  C I live to Madrid.

12
  A It's raining.
  B It rains.
  C It was cloudy.

13
  A It rained.
  B It rains.
  C It was rain.

14
  A the third of March
  B the three of March
  C three March

15
  A Yes, I do.
  B Yes, I can.
  C Yes, I have.

16
  A in 7 o'clock
  B on 7 o'clock
  C at 7 o'clock

17
  A I'm watching TV.
  B I watched TV.
  C I watch TV.

18
  A They are drinking coffee.
  B They are drink coffee.
  C They drink coffee.

19
  A Yes, of course.
  B Yes, I help you.
  C Yes, I do.

20
  A No, I didn't.
  B No, I don't.
  C No, I haven't.

21
  A No, I didn't go for holiday.
  B Yes, I went to the beach.
  C No, I haven't.

22
  A I enjoy swimming.
  B I enjoy to swim.
  C I enjoy to swimming.

23
  A I was watching television.
  B I watch television.
  C I watched television.

24
  A Sarah is the better student.
  B Sarah is best student.
  C Sarah is the best student.

25
  A London is bigger.
  B London is more bigger.
  C London is more big.

26
  A I have bought them last weekend.
  B I buy them last weekend.
  C I bought them last weekend.

27
  A twice a week
  B twice in the week
  C two times the week

28
  A I will visiting my Aunt.
  B I'm going for visit my Aunt.
  C I'm going to visit my Aunt.

29
  A Yes, once a week.
  B Yes, sometimes a week.
  C Yes, one time a week.

30
  A Yes, I went to Edinburgh last year.
  B Yes, I was in Cambridge.
  C Yes, I have gone to London.

31
  A Because I want to have a certificate.
  B Because of a certificate.
  C Because to have a certificate.

32
  A at about midday
  B I've had lunch.
  C Yes, I have had lunch.

33
  A Yes, there is much.
  B Yes, there is many.
  C Yes, there is a lot.

34
  A I was here since two years.
  B I've been here since two years.
  C I've been here for two years.

35
  A I am prefer dance music.
  B I am preferring dance music.
  C I prefer dance music.

36
  A I'm preferring to travel by car.
  B I prefer to travel by a car.
  C I prefer to travel by car.

37
  A I think to go for a coffee.
  B I think I will to go for a coffee.
  C I think I'll go for a coffee.

38
  A No, I've never had any.
  B No, I didn't.
  C No, I never tasted it.

39
  A since I was 12
  B for long time
  C since 5 years

40
  A two days before
  B two days ago
  C two days early

UNIT **1**

Festivals & special occasions

Vocabulary

1a Match the photos (A-H) with the festivals and special occasions (1-8).

1	Christmas	**5**	Halloween
2	Valentine's Day	**6**	New Year
3	a graduation	**7**	Carnival
4	a wedding	**8**	a birthday

b Think of all the other festivals and special occasions you can. Write them, and the ones in the pictures above, in the table.

British	national	international

1

2

3

4

5

2a In pairs, match the words from the box with each celebration. You may decide to put some words in more than one picture. Use a dictionary if you need to.

> rings carols bride & groom pumpkin
> lovers fireworks chocolates ghosts cards
> witches decorations resolutions presents
> Boxing Day midnight the best man roses

b Now use the definitions of seven words from a) to complete the crossword.

> midnight pumpkin cards chocolates
> decorations roses fireworks

Across

1 On New Year's Eve we stay up until this time.

3 We send these to friends and family at Christmas and on birthdays.

5 They are loud and colourful and we use them to celebrate special occasions.

6 They are sweet and we often eat them on special occasions, like Christmas.

7 This orange vegetable is popular at Halloween.

Down

2 People often put these up around the house at Christmas.

4 People give these flowers to say, 'I love you'.

c 🎧 **3** Listen to the four speakers. Which festival is each person describing?

3 Work in small groups, and choose a festival from this unit or another one from your country or region. Then follow these instructions.

1 List the things that people do and eat at this festival.

2 Expand the information by making notes about the items on your list.

3 Now one person from the group presents the festival to the rest of the class, without saying the name of the festival.

4 The rest of the class tries to name the festival.

9

Grammar focus

The Present Perfect

The Present Perfect is formed with *have/has* + the past participle (verb + *-ed*).
e.g. *She **has eaten** too much cake.*

In English, there are two main ways to talk about the past:
1 We use the **Past Simple** to talk about experiences with a **specific reference** to when the event happened. We use time expressions such as *yesterday, last week/month/year, in 1999, in January.*
*I **went** to Venice in 2006.*

2 We use the **Present Perfect** to talk about experiences when there is **no reference** to when the event happened. We use *for, since, ever, never* and *just.*
*I've **been** to Venice twice.*
*They've **celebrated** Carnival **for** hundreds of years.*
*She's **lived** in Hong Kong **since** 1998.*
*They've **never spent** New Year's Eve in Scotland.*
*They've **just come back** from holiday. (They were on holiday last week.)*
***Have** you **ever received** a Valentine's Day card?*

4 **Look at the sentences below and decide whether they contain the Present Perfect (A) or Past Simple (B).**

0 B I went to Edinburgh last year.
1 ☐ Jenny phoned Susan last night.
2 ☐ She has told us all the details.
3 ☐ Have you ever played basketball?
4 ☐ Brian has received a letter from Lia.
5 ☐ They opened their presents around the tree.
6 ☐ Emilio has never been to Venice.

5a **Look at these rules for using *for, since, ever, never* and *just* with the Present Perfect in English and complete them by putting the right word into each space. (Use the examples above to help you).**

We use...

1 .... when we want to focus on a period of time.

2 .... when we want to focus on the date or the time when a period began.

3 .... to emphasise that something has happened very recently.

4 .... when something has not happened at any time in the past.

5 .... when we want to ask questions about experiences in the past.

b Complete the following sentences using *for, since, ever, never* or *just*.

1 Have you .... seen a film starring Brad Pitt?

2 They've been in the football team .... last year.

3 I haven't seen Bruno .... ages!

4 She has .... moved to Madrid – her dad got a new job last month.

5 I've .... been to a film festival!

6 Have you .... been to a wedding?

c Go around the class asking questions beginning with *Have you ever...?* Try to find people who have done each of the activities in the list below.

Find someone who...

1 has eaten raw fish.   ....

2 has been to Greece.   ....

3 has been to an eighteenth birthday celebration.   ....

4 has seen a James Bond film.   ....

5 has been skiing.   ....

6 has played a musical instrument in public.   ....

d Now choose two of the activities above and ask more questions to find more information (use the box below to help you).

Remember!

We often begin conversations using the **Present Perfect** to ask about experiences. Then we may change to the **Past Simple** to continue talking about details of the experience.

A: *Have you ever been to London?*

B: *Yes, I have. In fact I've just been there.*

A: *When did you go there?*

B: *I went there last month.*

A: *Did you visit the Tower of London?*

B: *No, I didn't have time!*

Phonology

6a (4) Listen to these sentences with *have* in the Present Perfect. Do we use contractions in the positive, negative and interrogative forms?

1 I**'ve** been to Venice.

2 I **haven't** been to Venice.

3 **Have** you been to Venice? Yes, I **have**./No, I **haven't**.

b Practice saying these sentences with a partner.

1 They've finished their studies.

2 He's been to Paris.

3 Peter's gone shopping.

4 Yes, she has.

5 No, she hasn't.

6 Have you ever eaten roast beef?

7 I've been in the queue for hours!

8 She's just finished her shower.

c (5) Now listen to the sentences and repeat them.

Reading

7a Read this article about a festival and find out where it is.

b Say what these numbers from the text refer to.

1 825
2 three
3 six
4 1591
5 200

c Underline all the expressions that you can find in the article which refer to the past. Which tense is used? Why?

d Without looking at the text, work with a partner and tell them about the Bull Run in Pamplona. Use the following words in your sentences.

1 Pamplona bull run/happen/nearly every year since 1591
2 recent years/become/big tourist attraction
3 fire/rocket/confirm/gate/just open
4 you/ever/see/spectacle/this?

Writing

ISE Reading into Writing

→ *See Writing file on pages 78-91.*

8 Imagine that you went to the Pamplona Bull Run with some friends. Write a review (approximately 150 words) of your experience for a travel website:

i) describing what you saw **and**
ii) saying what you liked about it and what you didn't like.

THE BULL RUN

The bull run in Pamplona, northern Spain, has happened nearly every year since 1591. In recent years it has become a big tourist attraction. It takes place at 8 a.m. every morning from 7th to 14th July. Runners must be ready by 7.30 a.m. The actual run goes from the corral at Santo Domingo where the bulls are kept, to the bullring where they fight that same afternoon. The length of the run is 825 metres and the average time of the run from start to finish is about three minutes. The streets through the old town which make up the bull run are closed off, so the bulls can't escape. Each day six fighting bulls run the route.

The tension builds as the release of the bulls approaches and at 8 a.m. on the dot they fire a rocket to confirm that the gate has just opened at the Santo Domingo corral. The runners, who are dressed in white with a red handkerchief around their necks, pray to San Fermín. Then a second rocket announces that the bulls have left. The bulls and the runners then run along the route. Over 200 people have been seriously injured since 1924 during the run!

Have you ever seen a spectacle like this? No? Then start planning your trip!

Topic phase

◼ Preparing for the Topic phase

The Topic phase is the first part of the exam. You must prepare a topic before the exam to present to the examiner. This topic must not be from the list of subject areas from the Trinity syllabus.

9 **Complete this information about the Topic phase with the verbs in the box.**

> *prepare   learn   interests   remember   add*

Choosing my topic

Choose a topic that ¹................... you so that it is easy to speak about it. Make sure that you know, or can ²..................., enough grammar and vocabulary to be able to speak about it.

Preparing my topic

You must prepare a mind map with five discussion points on it. This will help you to ³................... what you want to say. You can also use notes and/or diagrams.

Do not memorise your topic! If the examiner thinks you have memorised it, she or he will automatically interrupt you.

Length of topic

The topic section of the exam is no more than 5 minutes. ⁴................... a presentation of not more than 2 minutes. The rest of the time will be a conversation with the examiner about your topic.

How to create a mind map

- Write the title of the topic in the middle of a piece of paper.
- ⁵................... ideas about the topic around the title.
- Then think of 3 or 4 sentences for each idea.
- Make sure you are using Grade 5 language as much as possible in your sentences.
- At least one of your sentences must be a question that you ask the examiner.

10a Peter is an English teacher in Mexico. He has prepared a short presentation about Christmas in England to give his class. Before you listen to Peter's topic presentation, tick (✓) the ideas in column A that you think he will include in his description of Christmas in Britain.

		A	B
1	special Christmas music	☐	☐
2	Christmas cards	☐	☐
3	visiting friends	☐	☐
4	excited children	☐	☐
5	the Christmas tree	☐	☐
6	watching television	☐	☐
7	eating too much	☐	☐
8	decorating the house	☐	☐

b 🎧 **6** Now listen to Peter and tick (✓) the ideas he talks about in column B. How many answers did you guess correctly?

c (6) **Listen to Peter again and decide whether the sentences below are true (T) or false (F).**

1 ☐ Peter doesn't like Christmas very much.
2 ☐ He normally celebrates Christmas with his family.
3 ☐ A Christmas tree must be a real tree.
4 ☐ Only the children get presents.
5 ☐ They open the presents round the tree.
6 ☐ They usually eat too much!

d Now look at the mind map that Peter has prepared, with the five discussion points for his presentation. Listen to his presentation again and add details for each discussion point, like in the example.

e Now make a mind map like Peter's to describe the most important festival of the year for you and your family.

Conversation phase

▨ Dos and don'ts

11 Complete the advice about the conversation phase by writing *Do* or *Don't* to start each sentence.

0 .....*Do*..... answer the question you are asked!

00 ..*Don't*.. just answer yes or no when the examiner asks you a question!

1 .... start an answer with *Let me think...*, or *Let's see...*, if you need extra time.

2 .... pause for too long before answering.

3 .... be prepared to give reasons for, or more details about, something you say.

4 .... remember that it's alright to talk about something ordinary – not having done something really exciting isn't an excuse for not talking!

5 .... ask the examiner at least one question in Grade 5, at least two in Grade 6 and for ISE I, one about the subject area and one for the portfolio. You could ask about the subject she/he has just asked you about.

6 .... show interest in and/or comment on the answer the examiner gives to your question/s, with expressions such as, *That sounds nice.*, *That sounds like fun.*, *How nice! Really?*

¹ The day itself
children very excited
open presents altogether
aunts, uncles and cousins come to visit

² Preparation for Christmas
....
....

³ Christmas tree
....
....

CHRISTMAS IN BRITAIN

⁴ What we eat
....
....

⁵ Christmas shopping
....
....

Writing

ISE Portfolio/CW

➡ *See Writing file on pages 78-91.*

12 Put the different stages (A-H) of doing a writing task into the correct order.

A ☐ Write a first draft.

B ☐ Listen to what your partner says about how you can improve your text.

C ☐ Write a plan for your text.

D ☐ Write a second draft.

E ☐ Give your text to your teacher.

F ☐ Swap texts with a partner and suggest ways for your partner to improve her/his text.

G ☐ Refer to exercises in this unit for help with subject area vocabulary and grammar.

H ☐ Refer to the Writing file for help with how to write the text type.

13 Choose one, or more, of these writing tasks.

Correspondence (*ISE I 2009*)

It is your cousin's 18th birthday soon. Her friend Jane has asked you what present she might like. Write an email to Jane saying what you think is a suitable gift and why. Say how your cousin is planning to celebrate her birthday. Write 70-80 words.

Factual writing (*ISE I 2007*)

You recently went to a music festival in your country. Write a review of the festival for a music magazine. Say what you thought about the different types of music, the performances and the atmosphere. Write 110-130 words.

Creative/descriptive writing

Write your diary for 1st January. Say how you celebrated New Year's Eve, describing who you were with and what you did. Write 110-130 words.

Trinity TAKE AWAY

Examiner: Is there a special festival in your town?
Candidate: Yes, we celebrate St Stephen's day – he's the Saint of our local church.
We parade through the streets and we have special St Stephen's cakes – they are really delicious. Have you tried one?

UNIT 2

Means of transport

A ....

B ....

C ....

D ....

E ....

F ....

Vocabulary

1a Label the pictures with a word from the box below.

> car helicopter train port minibus
> runway tram bicycle cruise ship bus
> coach underground airport taxi
> lighthouse ferry terminal

b Put the words from the box into the appropriate column of the table (some can go in more than one column). Use a dictionary to help you if you need to.

Air	
Sea	
Land	

Phonology

■ Intonation of basic question forms

2a (7) Listen to these two examples and notice the difference in the intonation.

1   What's your name? (▼)

2   Do you speak any other languages? (▲)

b (8) Now listen to these questions. Write them and decide if the end of the question goes up (▲) or down (▼).

1   ....

2   ....

3   ....

4   ....

5   ....

6   ....

(8) Listen to the questions again and repeat them using the same intonation.

Vocabulary

■ Transport survey

3a You are going to take part in a class survey on transport and travel. With a partner, practise asking and answering the questions below.

Questions about transport

How do you	usually normally	come get	to	school? university? class?

Answers about transport

I	come	on by	foot my bike/bicycle/motorbike/scooter car/bus/train/bike
I	take catch get	a the	bus/train/tram/underground

I get a lift	from with	my mother a friend

Questions about travel time

How long	does it take (you) do you take	to get to come	to	school? class?

Answers about travel time

It takes about half an hour.
It takes an hour if I'm lucky!
It depends on the traffic!

b Now work in groups and ask everyone in your group questions about how they travel every day. Note their answers on the survey record sheet below.

c When you have collected all your results and calculated the totals answer the following questions about your group.

1 What is the most popular form of transport?

2 What is the least popular form of transport?

3 Who has the quickest and who has the longest journey?

4 How many people travel by car? How many people travel by bike?

In your answers to these questions try to use expressions such as, *all of us*, *most of us*, *a lot of us*, *not very many of us* and *none of us*.

Reading

4a Read the explanation of 'no-frills' and conventional airlines. Then work with a partner. Ask and answer the questions below.

When you buy an airline ticket you are really paying simply to travel from one place to another. Conventional airlines usually give you a drink, a meal, a magazine or a newspaper to read. These are 'frills' – in other words, extra services. '**No-frills**' airlines often offer cheap tickets, but no extra services.

1 Have you ever travelled with a 'no-frills' airline?

2 If so, what was the journey like?

3 Would you recommend that airline to a friend?

b Read the text about 'no-frills' airlines and put the three headings below in the right place in the text. Decide which type of airline you prefer and talk to a partner about your reasons.

1 What won't you get?

2 What will you get with both 'no-frills' and conventional airlines?

3 What will you get with a 'no-frills' airline?

Name	....	....	....	....	....
walk					
bus					
tram					
underground					
train					
taxi					
lift					
drive a car					
motorbike					
bicycle					
journey time in minutes					
Total					

'NO-FRILLS' AIRLINES

In recent years there has been a revolution in the travel industry. The conventional airlines now face strong competition from a new generation of progressive airlines, so-called 'low-cost'. With their low **fares** and simple procedures these airlines are both taking business away from the conventional airlines and creating a new travel market of people who are encouraged to travel simply because low fares are available.

A ....

Well, you will get taken from one airport to another. You may not fly to the airports you would normally choose. They will probably be small and some way from the city they actually serve. You will also get a low, or in some cases, a very low, fare. You may find that people rush forward at the **boarding gate** to get their favourite seats on the plane.

B ....

Normally you won't get a choice of class – business or first class aren't usually available. You probably won't have a ticket. You will probably not be able **to book** your flight through a **travel agent**. You won't get any free snacks, drinks or meals. You probably won't get a choice between an a window and an **aisle seat**. You probably won't get an in-flight magazine or in-flight entertainment.

C ....

You will probably get a long **queue** at the **check-in desk**. You will run the risk of delays and losing your luggage!

c Match these definitions to the words or phrases highlighted in the text.

0 the place in the terminal where your ticket is checked   *check-in desk*

1 the place where you wait before you get on the plane   ....

2 another word for 'to reserve' a ticket   ....

3 the seat furthest from the window and closest to the centre   ....

4 a line of people   ....

5 the money that you pay in order to travel   ....

6 a person who organises travel and holidays   ....

d Look at the text again and then in pairs or small groups list the advantages and disadvantages of travel with a 'no-frills' airline.

Advantages	Disadvantages
cheap	airports may be far from city centres

Writing

ISE Reading into Writing

➡ *See Writing file on pages 78-91.*

5 Your teacher has proposed a class trip for a few days to another country. She has asked you to read about different ways to fly to the country she has chosen. Look again at the text about 'no-frills' airlines and write a report (about 150 words) for your teacher:

i) telling readers the advantages and disadvantages of 'no-frills' and conventional airlines **and**

ii) saying which type of airline you would prefer to use and why.

Grammar focus

Will referring to the future

Forming the future with *will*
The future with *will* is formed by adding *will* to the base form of the verb (infinitive without *to*).
I + will + go   I + will not (won't) + go

In speech and informal writing we normally contract the subject with *will*.

I will → I'll   you will → you'll   we will → we'll

Using *will* for the future
Will has many different meanings for future reference.
Two of these are predicting and informing about the future.

1 Predicting
*I think I'll **finish** my degree next year.*
*I'll probably **be** a lawyer when I finish my studies.*

2 Informing
*The journey to Brighton **will take** two hours.*
*We **won't be able to** buy tickets on the bus.*

We often use *will* to make predictions with words
like *probably* and after verbs which indicate
a decision or judgement.
*I'll **probably take** the train to work tomorrow.*
*I **think I'll take** a holiday next week.*
*I'm **sure you'll be** here in time for dinner.*
*I **imagine they'll win** easily.*

6a **Here are some questions about the future
with possible answers. Try to match the
questions (1-5) with the right answers (A-F).**

0 [A] What do you plan to do after your
studies?

1 [ ] What are Emilio's plans for university?

2 [ ] What do you hope to do this weekend?

3 [ ] What job does Emilio **not** want to do?

4 [ ] What will you do if there's nothing on
TV tonight?

5 [ ] Is there a particular programme you
want to see?

A I'll probably become a teacher.

B He won't be a bus driver!

C He'll probably study town planning.

D In that case I'll read or go to bed early.

E Yes, the football – I'm sure we'll win!

F I'll probably go to the cinema.

b **Complete the tour guide's information using a
will future for informing and the verbs below.**

> *include   take   leave   be*

'Good morning everyone. We would like to
inform you of one or two changes to our
programme for tomorrow. The bus tour of the
city centre [1].............. the hotel at 9.45, but don't
worry, you [2].............. back at the hotel in time for
dinner at 6 p.m. The tour [3].............. about five hours
and [4].............. a stop for lunch in the old part of the
city. We hope you have a pleasant trip!'

c **Think about transport in your town/city. What
do you think will be the major problems in
the next decade? Complete the sentences
below with your ideas.**

1 I think...   **3** I imagine...

2 I'm sure...   **4** ...will probably...

**Now exchange ideas with the person next to
you. Do you agree or disagree?**

Topic phase

■ Preparing and presenting your topic

7a Look at this photo of Turin. What types of transport can you see? Compare it with your own city or home town. What is different? What is the same? Talk about this with a partner.

b 🎧**9** Emilio is a Grade 5 candidate from Turin. He has decided to make 'Transport in Turin' his topic and you will hear him presenting his topic to an examiner. Look at Emilio's Topic form for the exam. Listen to the recording and number the points on the form in the order in which you hear Emilio talking about them.

c 🎧**9** Listen again and decide whether these statements are true (T) or false (F).

1. ☐ There are many different types of transport in Turin.
2. ☐ Emilio has just moved to Turin.
3. ☐ Turin has an underground railway.
4. ☐ Some public transport in Turin is environmentally friendly.
5. ☐ Emilio doesn't want to be a bus driver.

d Now talk to a partner and decide whether you would like to visit Turin. Is it like your home town?

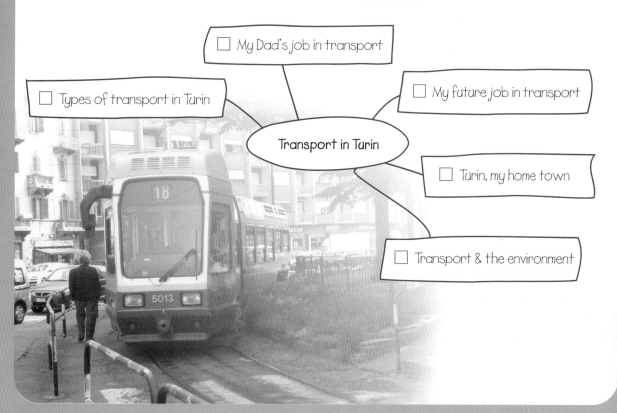

☐ My Dad's job in transport

☐ Types of transport in Turin

☐ My future job in transport

Transport in Turin

☐ Turin, my home town

☐ Transport & the environment

exam expert

8a Emilio made extra mind maps to help him prepare his topic. Each mind map gives information about the main discussion points on his Topic form. Look at the extra information about Turin below.

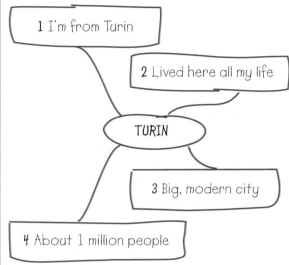

1 I'm from Turin

2 Lived here all my life

TURIN

3 Big, modern city

4 About 1 million people

b 🎧 **9** Listen to Emilio's presentation again and as you listen, complete the extra mind maps below to give more information about the other discussion points.

c 🎧 **10** Remember! Don't memorise your presentation. Listen to the same topic presentation, this time the candidate has memorised it. What differences are there between the two versions? What do you notice about the candidate's intonation?

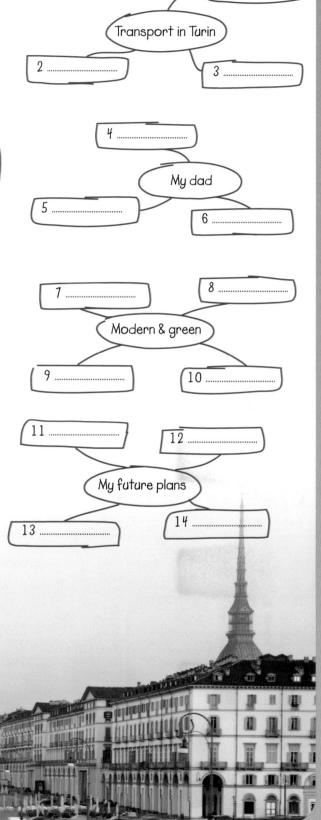

1 ....

Transport in Turin

2 ....

3 ....

4 ....

My dad

5 ....

6 ....

7 ....

8 ....

Modern & green

9 ....

10 ....

11 ....

12 ....

My future plans

13 ....

14 ....

9 Complete these sentences about the Topic phase with *do* and *don't*.

Topic 'Do's and Don'ts'

1 .... memorise your topic! It may make you feel more confident but it will almost certainly spoil your pronunciation. In any case, the examiner will interrupt you!

2 .... practise using your mind map to remind you of what you planned to say.

3 .... link the points you are making together.

E.g. 'I come from Turin *and* I've lived here all my life. It's a big, modern city *with* a population of about a million people.'

4 .... remember – you must ask the examiner at least one question.

E.g. 'Have you ever been to Turin?'

5 .... be surprised if the examiner asks you to talk about your topic in a different order than you've put on your mind map.

Writing

ISE Portfolio/CW

➡ *See Writing file on pages 78-91.*

10 Choose one, or more, of these Writing Tasks.

Correspondence (*ISE I 2010*)

You recently got a new mountain bike for your birthday. Write a letter to your English pen friend saying how long you have had it, what you have to do to keep it in good condition and why you enjoy riding it. Write 70-80 words.

Factual writing (*ISE I 2007*)

Write an article for a travel guide about the different ways of travelling around your country. Describe the different methods of transport available and say which one is the best value for money. Say how you prefer to travel and why. Write 110-130 words.

Creative/descriptive writing (*ISE I 2009*)

Write a story for a writing competition which starts with the words, 'If I have to go on a long journey again, I definitely won't travel by bus'. Write 110-130 words.

Examiner: How do you normally travel to your classes?
Candidate: Well, it depends on the weather. It only takes me 20 minutes to walk to school, but if it's raining, my mother gives me a lift.

UNIT 3

Entertainment & music

Vocabulary

■ Music

1a Match these instruments (1-10) to the pictures (A-J).

1	accordion	**6**	trumpet
2	keyboard	**7**	trombone
3	violin	**8**	drums
4	piano	**9**	guitar
5	organ	**10**	saxophone

b Do you know the names for the people who play these instruments? Put them in the right columns below.

-ist	-er	- player
accordionist	trumpeter	keyboard-player

c Work with a partner and take turns to ask and answer these questions.

1 Can you play a musical instrument? If so, which one?

2 Does any of your family or friends play an instrument?

3 Which instrument do you like listening to?

4 Do you prefer playing music or listening to music?

d Work with a partner and talk about music using the following example to help you.

A: Do you play a musical instrument?

B: No, I don't but my *sister's/father's/cousin's a guitarist/pianist/keyboard player/violinist.* And how about you? Do you play an instrument?

Or

B: Yes, I do. I play the piano. And how about you? Do you play an instrument?

A: No, I don't – I haven't got the patience to practise!

2a Do you know all these different types of music? Match the type with the musician.

1	☐	hip hop	**A**	Beethoven
2	☐	rap	**B**	Lady Gaga
3	☐	classical	**C**	Linkin Park
4	☐	pop	**D**	Shakira
5	☐	folk	**E**	Eminem
6	☐	new metal	**F**	Bob Marley
7	☐	reggae	**G**	Bob Dylan
8	☐	dance	**H**	The Black Eyed Peas

b Now talk about music with your partner. Ask and answer the following questions.

1 What kind of music do you like?

2 Do you ever listen to any of the musicians in a)?

3 When do you usually listen to music?

4 Have you ever been to a live concert or a music festival?

UNIT 3

■ Film

3a How well do you know British films? Work in pairs and see how many answers you know to this quiz – if you don't know an answer, guess!

b Now work with another pair. Did you get the same answers? If not, decide which are the correct answers. Then, go to page 92 and check your answers.

c Look at these adjectives to describe films, books and TV programmes. Decide whether they are used to say you like the entertainment or you don't.

> boring dull exciting entertaining
> predictable moving funny fascinating
> beautiful slow silly interesting
> romantic great awful

Did you like the film?

No, it was really...

Yes, it was really...

d Now work in pairs. Use the adjectives from c) to describe a TV programme or a film you have seen recently.

Lights, Camera, Action! – a film quiz

1 The stars of *Notting Hill* were
  A Hugh Grant & Gwyneth Paltrow.   **B** Hugh Grant & Julia Roberts.   **C** Brad Pitt & Julia Roberts.

2 In the Harry Potter films, Harry's best friend is called
  A Hermione.   **B** Geraldine.   **C** Voldemort.

3 Renee Zellwegger starred in a film called *Bridget Jones's*
  A *Journal*.   **B** *Diary*.   **C** *Confessions*.

4 *Slumdog Millionaire* took place in
  A Scotland.   **B** The United States.   **C** India.

5 *Billy Elliot* was a film about
  A football.   **B** a famous jazz singer.
  C a boy who wants to be a ballet dancer.

6 In *Bend It Like Beckham*, the protagonist wants to become
  A a singer.   **B** a footballer.   **C** an actress.

7 *Sherlock Holmes* was directed by
  A David Lynch.   **B** Martin Scorsese.   **C** Guy Ritchie.

8 How many Oscars did *Shakespeare in Love* win?
  A 7   **B** 3   **C** 1

Grammar focus

Expressing preferences

There are several ways of talking about preferences in English. Here are two of them.

1 Talking about your preferences in general.

prefer + object + to + object
She **prefers** original versions **to** films with subtitles.

subject + prefer + + verb + -ing + to + verb + -ing
I **prefer** swimming **to** running

In conversation, the questions which would produce answers like these would be:
Which actor do you prefer – Gwyneth Paltrow or Julia Roberts?
What does she prefer – playing music or listening to it?

2 Talking about preferences on a specific occasion.
+ would ('d) rather + infinitive without to + than + infinitive without to
I**'d rather** go to Salsa classes **than** go to the gym.
He**'d rather** see Sherlock Holmes *again* **than** watch a romantic film.

In conversation, the questions which would produce answers like these would be:
What would you rather do – buy the CD or go to the concert?
What would you rather do – read a book or see a film?

4a Use the promts to make sentences using *prefer*.

0 I/Pierce Brosnan/Brad Pitt
  I prefer Pierce Brosnan to Brad Pitt

1 Giuseppe/play/music/listen/to it
2 She/Scarlett Johansson/Halle Berry
3 We/action films/romantic films
4 My mother/romantic novels/science fiction
5 They/go/cinema/watch DVDs

b Work in pairs. Ask and answer questions using the prompts below.

1 What/prefer/classical concerts/rock concerts?
2 Who/prefer/Robert Pattinson/Daniel Radcliffe?
3 What/prefer/visting/art galleries/museums?
4 Who/prefer/Rihanna/Lilly Allen?

c Now, think of three questions like these about entertainment to ask your partner, using the structures above.

5a Use the promts to make sentences using *rather*.

0 I/buy/CD/go/concert
  I'd rather buy a CD than go to a concert

1 They/read/book/see/film
2 He/meet/friends/do/homework
3 I/play football/watch it
4 My father/stay/home/go/party
5 She/travel for a year/go straight to University

b Work in pairs. Ask and answer questions, using the prompts below.

1 What/rather/go/classical concert/rock concert?

2 What/rather/watch TV/listen/music?

3 What/rather/see/film/go/restaurant?

4 What/rather/go/walk/watch/DVD?

c Now, think of three questions like these about entertainment to ask your partner.

Phonology

▨ Intonation of more complex question forms

6a (11) Listen to these three questions asking about preferences. The arrows below show the direction of the speaker's voice.

1 Would you like tea or coffee?

2 Do you prefer Rihanna or Lilly Allen?

3 Would you rather go to the cinema or the theatre?

b (11) Now listen to the questions again and repeat them using the same intonation.

c In pairs, write questions using the prompts below. Student A should ask the questions and Student B should answer them. Pay particular attention to the intonation.

1 pop music/classical music

2 adventure films/romantic films

3 Christmas/New Year

4 cars/motorbikes

5 studying/shopping

Listening

7a (12) Listen to Peter and Maria talking about what entertainment they like and what they don't like. As you listen, complete the table below by putting a tick (✓) in the column for Peter or for Maria.

		Peter	Maria
1	watches TV a lot	☐	☐
2	prefers going out to staying in	☐	☐
3	loves live music	☐	☐
4	prefers classical music to pop music	☐	☐
5	goes to the cinema once or more a week	☐	☐
6	is fond of romantic films	☐	☐
7	hates romantic films	☐	☐
8	sometimes prefers to stay at home with a DVD	☐	☐

b Here are a number of expressions for saying how much you like or hate something. Put them in order from the most positive (1) to the most negative (6).

A ☐ I can't stand...

B ☐ I can't get enough of...

C ☐ I really love...

D ☐ I'm quite fond of...

E ☐ ...leaves me cold!

F ☐ I don't mind...

c (12) Now listen to Peter and Maria again. Tick (✓) the expressions in b) which they use.

d Work in pairs. Use the expressions from b) to talk about the types of entertainment that you like and don't like. Do you and your partner have similar tastes?

Reading

8a Work in pairs. Ask each other about what type of concert you most enjoy. Ask when your partner last went to a concert, and who was playing. Ask what your partner thought about the concert.

b Peter went to a concert recently and afterwards posted a short review of the concert on his blog. Read his review and find out what type of music was played.

c Now answer these questions.

   1 Where was the concert?

   2 What time did the concert start and finish?

   3 Would Peter recommend the concert?

Writing

ISE Reading into Writing

9a Now practise writing a review by answering the questions to complete the spaces below. You can make it as positive or as negative as you like!

b Read the text again and then, in your own words, write an email (approximately 150 words) to your English speaking friend:

   i) telling her/him about the Brighton Festival singers' concert you went to and

   ii) explaining which type of music you liked best.

From Bach to the Beatles

Last night the Brighton Festival Singers gave a concert at All Saints Church. The concert began at 8.00 p.m. and finished at 10.00, with a short interval. They were conducted by John Makepiece, who has conducted many major choirs in several European countries. The programme included works by Bach, Elvis Presley and the Beatles – as you can imagine there was something for everyone! The quality of the singing was very high and two pieces were accompanied beautifully by 18- year-old Jenny Wilkins on the piano. I really loved every minute! The choir was established in 1987 and consists of local singers who meet weekly to rehearse and prepare performances. Take the opportunity to go to their next performance!

Last night the group of the moment *(What was the name of the group?)* **1**.. performed at *(Where was the concert?)* **2**.. . The concert lasted for *(How long did they play for?)* **3**.. and they played all their hits, including *(What is the name of one of their hits?)* **4**.. .

(Name of the group) **5**.. are from *(Where are they from?)* **6**.. . There are *(How many people are there in the group?)* **7**.. members in the group. The music they play is *(What type of music do they play?)* **8**.. . The atmosphere at the concert was *(What was the atmosphere like?)* **9**.. and the audience *(What did the audience think of it?)* **10**.. . The best part of last night's concert was *(What was the best part of the concert?)* **11**.., but the worst part was *(What was the worst part?)* **12**.. . Overall the concert *(Was it a success?)* **13**.. and I thought *(What did you think about it?)* **14**.. . In fact, *(Would you recommend it?)* **15**.. .

exam expert

Topic phase

▨ Responding to the examiner

The interview is divided into the following 4 parts:

> **Greetings** and settling in

> Presentation and discussion of your topic (**Topic phase**)

> **Conversation** on two subject areas (Grades 5 & 6)

> **Ending** and saying goodbye

Before you start your topic presentation, the examiner will greet you, ask to see your photo identification and ask a few questions.

▨ Asking the examiner questions

Be prepared to ask the examiner questions in the exam. At Grade 5 ask the examiner one question in the Topic phase and one question in the Conversation phase.

It is a good idea to prepare some possible questions to ask the examiner about your topic.

10a Match these questions and instructions (1-6) to the appropriate responses (A-F).

1. ☐ Please sit down.
2. ☐ What's your name?
3. ☐ How do you spell *Huang*?
4. ☐ How are you?
5. ☐ Have you ever taken one of these exams before?
6. ☐ Can I have your Topic form, please?

A Lian Huang
B Fine thanks, and you?
C H-U-A-N-G
D Yes, of course. Here you are.
E Yes. I did grade 3 last year.
F Thank you.

b Now ask and answer the questions in a) with a partner.

11a Look at these example topic presentation titles and think of two possible questions that you could ask the examiner for each one.

0 Football in Spain
    Is football popular in your country?
    Do you like watching football?

1 My home town
    ....
    ....

2 My trip to London
    ....
    ....

3 The Scouts
    ....
    ....

4 Canoeing
    ....
    ....

5 Transport in my city
    ....
    ....

b Now write two questions that you could ask the examiner about your chosen topic.

Conversation phase

■ Exam practice

12a Match the questions (1-8) that an examiner might ask you about music and entertainment to suitable answers (A-I).

0 ☑D Do you like listening to classical music?

1 ☐ What type of films do you like watching?

2 ☐ How often do you go to the cinema?

3 ☐ Do you prefer watching films on TV or at the cinema?

4 ☐ Who is your favourite singer?

5 ☐ Can you recommend a film you have seen recently?

6 ☐ What is your favourite TV programme?

7 ☐ How much TV do you watch every day?

8 ☐ Would you rather listen to pop music or reggae?

A I prefer watching films on the big screen.

B I like romantic films.

C I think Amy Winehouse is very talented.

D Yes, I love it.

E at least once a month

F I like watching N.C.I.S.

G about 2 hours a day

H Yes, *Inception* is really good.

I I'd rather listen to reggae!

b With a partner, ask each other the questions above and give your own answers.

c Now think of a question that you could ask the examiner about music and entertainment.

Writing

ISE Portfolio/CW

➡ *See Writing file on pages 78-91.*

13 Choose one, or more, of these Writing Tasks.

Correspondence (*ISE I 2009*)

You have two tickets to see your favourite band in concert. Write an email to a friend inviting her to go to the concert with you. Say when and where the concert will take place and explain why you think your friend will enjoy it. Write 70-80 words.

Factual writing (*ISE I 2009*)

A new disco has recently opened in your area. Write a review for an entertainment guide giving your opinion on the music and atmosphere. Say how successful you think the disco will be. Write 110-130 words.

Creative/descriptive writing (*ISE I 2011*)

Write a story for a music magazine about four teenagers who formed a band and appeared on television. Explain what music the band played, what they had to do on television and how it helped them become famous. Write 110-130 words.

Trinity TAKE AWAY

Examiner: Can you play a musical instrument?
Candidate: No – but **I really love** listening to all types of music. How about you – are you a musician, or **do you prefer** other forms of entertainment?

UNIT **4**

Recent personal experiences

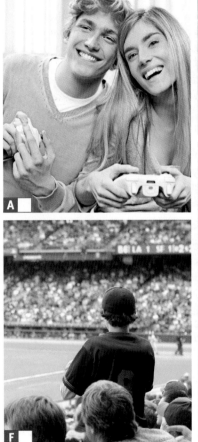

Vocabulary

1a **Match the photos (A-H) with the activities (1-8) they show.**

1 seeing friends
2 celebrating a special occasion
3 studying
4 playing video games
5 watching sport
6 going away for the weekend/on holiday
7 playing sport
8 going to a concert

b **Tick (✓) three activities you like doing. Put a cross (✗) next to three you don't like doing. Compare your answers with a partner.**

E.g. **A:** I really like going away for the weekend. What about you?

B: Yes, me too, especially in summer, to the beach. And I love going shopping! But I don't like watching sport. What about you?

A: Well, I don't like watching football, but I quite like watching tennis.

■ Past time expressions

2a Read the posts from a social networking site about recent activities. Which activity from exercise 1a) does each person write about?

Alex writes:
I played in a match for the school team yesterday afternoon and we lost, 5-nil! We lost the weekend before last, too, by 6-nil! I think we need to train harder!

Ana writes:
I had such a great weekend! It was my mum's birthday last Saturday and we held a surprise party for her. It was so much fun! Check out the photos.

Jie writes:
They're over! I've finally finished. I did the last one yesterday. No more exams and no school for two months! All I've done for the past two weeks is revise! Now I can have some fun!

Shirin writes:
I want to live by the sea! We got back to town two hours ago, after a fantastic time at the beach. I miss it already!

Luca writes:
If you weren't there last night, you missed a fantastic experience.
I think they played every song they've ever recorded. It was the best gig I've been to for ages.

b Underline the expressions relating to past time in the posts in exercise 2a).

c Complete the past time expressions in the table below using a word from the phrases you underlined in b).

d Jie uses the expression 'for two months' and Luca says 'for ages'. Does each person refer to the past, present or future? Can these expressions be used with other tenses?

3 Work with a partner. Ask and answer at least five questions about activities you've done recently. Use the expressions in the table below, where possible.

A: So, what did you do last night?

B: Nothing! I was so tired after last weekend, I went to bed at 9 o'clock!

A: Did you do anything last Saturday night?

B: Yes, actually, I went to a concert. It was great...

> **Remember!**
>
> *I've finished my exams!*
> Use the Present Perfect to talk about events at an unspecified time in the past.
>
> *I did my French exam yesterday.*
> Use the Past Simple to talk about events that happened at a specified time in the past.
>
> For more information on the use of the Present Perfect and Past Simple, see **Unit 1 page 10**.

	night/week/weekend/month/year	
1	Monday/Tuesday/Wednesday...	
the **2** ..../...................	two days/week/two weeks/two months/year	
the day/weekend/week/year	before **3**	
4	morning/afternoon/evening	
two/three/four...	hours/days/weeks/months/years	**5** ....

Phonology

■ *-ed* past tense endings

4a Put the past tense forms in bold in these sentences from exercise 2a) into the correct column, according to the pronunciation of the *-ed* ending.

I **played** in a match for the school team yesterday afternoon and we lost, 5-nil!

They're over! I've finally **finished**.

I think they played every song they've ever **recorded**.

1	2	3
/t/	/d/	/ɪd/
	played	

b 🔊(13) Listen to check, then listen and repeat.

c 🔊(14) Now put these past tense forms into the correct columns. Listen to check, then listen and repeat.

> missed visited danced watched celebrated
> arrived decided wanted talked relaxed
> enjoyed loved worked waited

5a Work with a partner to invent a story.

- Use as many of the past verb forms from exercise 4c) as you can.
- Make notes, but don't write the story in full.
- Practise telling the story – remember the *-ed* endings!

b Change partners and tell your new partner your story.

- Count how many past verb forms from exercise 4c) your partner uses.
- Check your partner's pronunciation of the past tense verb forms.

Reading

6a Tick (✓) things (1-5) that you've bought and things (A-E) that you've done in the past six months. Then compare with a partner.

I've bought...

1 ☐ new clothes.
2 ☐ a computer.
3 ☐ an MP3 player.
4 ☐ a mobile phone.
5 ☐ a video game.

I've been...

A ☐ on holiday.
B ☐ to an adventure park.
C ☐ for a meal at a restaurant.
D ☐ to the cinema.
E ☐ to visit a new place.

b What makes you feel happy? When you buy something, when you do something, or both? Compare your opinion with a partner.

DOING OR BUYING?

A trip to an adventure park or a new MP3 player? A meal at a restaurant or a new pair of jeans? A smart new computer or a holiday? What would you choose?

Well, a study carried out in the USA by the University of Colorado has found that people are happier if they spend money on life experiences, rather than material possessions. Through a series of surveys and experiments over several years, researchers found that people from various social groups were happier when they spent money on doing things, rather than buying things.

One of the reasons suggested for this in the study is that experiences are more open to positive interpretations. For example, imagine you go on

a holiday and the weather or accommodation is not very good. Maybe you feel disappointed at the time, but later on, perhaps you'll change your view and start to think of the positive aspects of the experience – the new food you tried, or the new places that you saw. With material things, you can't reinterpret in this way because they are what they are – their qualities don't change.

Another possible reason why experiences bring more joy than material goods is that experiences also help us build up better social relationships. We tend to do things with other people, and we often share stories about the things we've done, so there is a social aspect to experiences that material possessions just don't have. And social success is closely associated with happiness.

7a Read the text above and answer these questions.

1 Is the text from
   A ☐ a science text book?
   B ☐ an article in newspaper or magazine?
   C ☐ an online advertisement?

2 What makes people the happiest, according to the article?
   A ☐ buying things
   B ☐ spending money
   C ☐ doing things

b Read the text again. Write T (true) or F (false) for each statement?

1 ☐ Research for the study took place in different countries.

2 ☐ The study lasted for a few months.

3 ☐ Lots of different kinds of people took part in the study.

4 ☐ According to the study, you can't change your opinion about experiences, but you can about material things.

5 ☐ According to the study, experiences help us develop socially, and this makes us happier.

8 Work with a partner. Tell her/him about:

1 a disappointing experience – how you felt at the time and how you felt later

2 something you've bought that made you feel really happy

3 something you've done with other people that's helped you socially.

Grammar focus

Connecting clauses

We can connect clauses using words such as *because*, *but*, *so* and *also*. Look at these examples from the text and notice how the connecting words in bold are used.

A *Maybe you feel disappointed at the time, **but** later on, you may change your view...*
B *With material things, you can't reinterpret in this way **because** they are what they are...*
C *...experiences **also** help us build up better social relationships.*
D *...we often share stories about the things we've done, **so** there is a social aspect to experiences...*

9a Now match the sentences (A-D) to the explanations (1-4) about the use of the connecting word in each sentence.

1 ☐ to give reasons
2 ☐ to add a point
3 ☐ to make a contrasting point
4 ☐ to talk about results or consequences

b Match the beginnings (1-4) with the endings (A-D) to make sentences.

1 ☐ People like doing things with other people. They
2 ☐ Buying things can make people happy,
3 ☐ I'm not very happy with my new mobile phone
4 ☐ I spend all my time at work on a computer,

A because it's complicated to use.
B but doing things makes them happier.
C so I don't even want to check my email at weekends!
D also like talking about what they've done.

c Complete the sentences with a connecting word from the grammar focus.

1 I bought a new mobile phone .... my old one was broken.
2 We went to London last week and we .... went to Brighton.
3 My mum thinks this video game is too violent, ... she's taking it back to the shop.
4 Angela enjoyed the holiday, ... she didn't like the food very much.
5 I haven't got much money, ... I can't go on holiday this summer.

d Complete these sentences in your own words, then compare with a partner.

1 I like/don't like .... because
....
2 My favourite time of year is ....
because ....
3 I really like/don't really like ....
because ....
4 I'm happiest when I'm .... because
....

Writing

ISE Reading into Writing

➡ *See Writing files on pages 78-91.*

10 Read the text on page 35 again, then, in your own words, write an article (approximately 150 words) to post on a blog about experiences, material possessions and happiness. Tell readers about the reasons the study gives to explain the findings, and give your own personal examples.

Conversation phase

■ Showing understanding of the examiner

11a 🎧(15) **Listen to the examiner and candidate talking in the Conversation phase. What event is the conversation about?**

b 🎧(15) **Listen again and tick (✓) the things that the examiner asks about.**

0	✓	activities/entertainment
1	☐	location of the candidate's house
2	☐	the candidate's family
3	☐	transport
4	☐	traffic problems
5	☐	food and meals
6	☐	details of the journey/s
7	☐	the candidate's friends
8	☐	the weather

c Match the examiner's questions to the things in b).

A	☐ 0	So, have you done anything special recently?
B	☐	Where is the house exactly?
C	☐	How did you get there?
D	☐	What time did you get there?
E	☐	So was the weather good?
F	☐	Did you go to the beach?
G	☐	So what did you do?
H	☐	And did you do anything on the Saturday night?
I	☐	So, did you go back home on Sunday evening?

d 🎧(15) **Now match the candidate's answers to the questions in c). Then listen to the conversation again to check.**

0	C	By car – and it took ages because the traffic was so bad.
1	☐	Yeah, we left at about 5 o'clock and the traffic was terrible again!
2	☐	Let me think. Oh yes, the weekend before last, I went away with my family...
3	☐	It's on the south-west coast, in a small village, about 200 km from here.
4	☐	Really late – I think it was about midnight, so we went straight to bed.
5	☐	Well, I played beach ball with my brother... I... read a book... I ate lots of ice cream!
6	☐	Yeah, I went out for dinner with my family, then I met some friends...
7	☐	Oh yes, it was beautiful – really hot and sunny all weekend.
8	☐	Yes, we spent most of Saturday and Sunday on the beach. But I didn't swim very much because the sea was so cold.

e 🎧(15) **The candidate asks the examiner a question. Listen to the end of the conversation again and complete the question.**

And .... you – have you been .... for the .... recently?

f Use words and phrases from the box to make other questions that the candidate could ask the examiner. You can use some words and phrases more than once.

> *Did you   anything special recently?*
> *travel here by plane?   D/do you   driving?*
> *like   What's   going to the beach?*
> *the weather   where you live?   Where*
> *live exactly?   the traffic   Have you*
> *done   lived in another country?*

E.g.   Did you travel here by plane?

12a Read a candidate's answers to some questions about recent personal experience and write some other questions the examiner could ask.

1 I went away with my family last weekend.
   Who exactly did you go with?
   Where did you go?

2 I went to India on holiday last summer.

3 I went shopping last weekend.

4 I had exams at school last week.

5 I visited an old friend the day before yesterday.

6 We celebrated my grandmother's birthday last month.

b Work with a partner. Have short conversations by asking each other your questions from exercise 12a) and inventing answers.

A: *I went away with my family last weekend.*
B: *Really? Where did you go?*
A: *We went skiing in Scotland.*
B: *How nice!*

Conversation phase

▨ Exam practice

13 Student A read the examiner rolecard and Student B read the candidate rolecard. Follow the instructions.

Student A: Examiner	Student B: Candidate
Stage 1 Prepare questions to ask the candidate about a recent personal experience.	**Stage 1** Think of something you've done recently and prepare to give details about it.
• Refer back to 11c) and 12a) for help with questions.	• Refer back to 11d) and 12a) for help.
Stage 2 Have the conversation with Student B/the candidate.	**Stage 2** Have the conversation with Student A/the examiner.
Stage 3 Decide with Student B what went well in the conversation and what you could improve. Your teacher will also give you some ideas.	**Stage 3** Decide with Student A what went well in the conversation and what you could improve. Your teacher will also give you some ideas.
Stage 4 Now change roles and repeat stages 1-3.	**Stage 4** Now change roles and repeat stages 1-3.

Writing

ISE Portfolio/CW

➡ *See Writing files on pages 78-91.*

14 Follow the stages (A-H) to practise writing tasks about recent personal experiences for the ISE I exam. Choose one, or more, of these writing tasks.

A Refer to the Writing file for help with how to write the text type.

B Refer to exercises in this unit for help with subject-area vocabulary and grammar.

C Write a plan for your text.

D Write a first draft.

E Swap texts with a partner and suggest ways for your partner to improve her/his text.

F Listen to what your partner says about how you can improve your text.

G Write a second draft.

H Give your text to your teacher.

Correspondence *(ISE I 2010)*

You have just won a prize in a talent show for your singing. Write an email to a friend saying what you have won, what you had to do to get the prize and when you are planning to perform in the future. Write 70-80 words.

Factual writing *(ISE I 2010)*

Write a report for your school magazine about social networking sites as a way of telling friends about your life and experiences. Talk about the advantages and disadvantages of this way of contacting with people. Write 110-130 words.

Creative/descriptive writing *(ISE I 2008)*

Write your diary (true or imaginary) for a day when you had the opportunity to do something you have always wanted to do. Write 110-130 words.

Examiner: Have you done anything special recently?
Candidate: Yes, the **weekend before last**, I went away with my family **because** it was my mother's birthday. The weather was beautiful **so** we spent a lot of time outside.

1 The groups of letters below can be rearranged to make words we have used in the first two units. The first one has been done for you. Then, match the words to the definitions.

0 laminter   terminal ....

1 atunigorda   ....

2 sontulieros   ....

3 cyliceb   ....

4 yawnur   ....

5 yaBgniDox   ....

6 derbi   ....

A ☐ The ceremony that you attend when you have finished your studies at university.

B ☐ The word we use to describe a woman on her wedding day.

C ☐ The place where aircraft take off or land.

D ☐ *O* The part of an airport where you find check-in desks, shops, restaurants etc.

E ☐ The promises that you make at the beginning of a New Year.

F ☐ The day after Christmas Day.

G ☐ Simple transport for one person with two wheels.

2 Here are a number of sentences. Some are right but some have a mistake in them. If you find a mistake, write the corrected sentence.

1 They are in Paris since last week.

2 I've been in this queue for hours!

3 I've seen him at the wedding last Saturday.

4 I play the guitar but I've never played it in public.

5 When I finished my studies I probably become a teacher.

6 The flight to Madrid will probably take two hours.

3 Use these words to make good sentences – you will need to add or change some words.

1 the Bull Run/Pamplona/happen/every year/1951

2 rocket/announce/bulls/leave

3 you/ever/eat/octopus?

4 often/travel/train?

5 she/just/finish/homework

6 I/probably/become/doctor/when/older

7 I/certain/they/arrive/here/an hour

8 I/go/Tokyo/1999/but/not be/there again

4 Look again at the pictures of musical instruments on page 24. Now list the instruments in the table below next to the correct type of music. You can put some instruments in more than one row.

Jazz	
Pop	
Classical	
Folk	

5 Using some of the adjectives from the box on page 26, complete these sentences.

1 The film was really ....! In fact I thought it was never going to end!

2 It was the most .... film I've ever seen! I was sitting on the edge of my seat from the start to the finish!

3 She prefers .... films – you know, the type where a man falls in love with a woman and they are very happy!

4 I found the film really ....! I could guess exactly how it was going to end!

6 In the following sentences we have offered you two choices. Underline the correct word or phrase.

1 At last *I finished/I've finished* my exams. Now I'm free!

2 She prefers *swimming to skiing/to swim than to ski*.

3 I'd rather *to go/go* to the cinema.

4 She *visited/has visited* Turkey last year.

5 *Did you do/Have you done* anything special recently?

7 Read the information about the exam, and decide if they refer to the Topic phase (T), the Conversation phase (C), or both (TC).

1 ☐ It is the first part of the exam.

2 ☐ It lasts up to 5 minutes.

3 ☐ You must ask the examiner at least one question.

4 ☐ You mustn't memorise what you are going to say.

5 ☐ You must prepare a mind map with five discussion points on it.

6 ☐ It involves two subject areas.

Grade 5 Self-evaluation

Write Y (yes) or N (needs more practice) for each statement.

1 ☐ I can talk about festivals and celebrations.

2 ☐ I can talk about transport.

3 ☐ I can talk about films and entertainment.

4 ☐ I can talk about my preferences.

5 ☐ I can use the Present Perfect and Past Simple to talk about my experiences.

6 ☐ I can talk about the future using *will* for predicting and informing.

7 ☐ I can use words and phrases to connect clauses correctly.

UNIT **5**

Fashion
& money

Vocabulary

▨ Fashion

1a Label each picture with an expression from the box.

> high fashion   extreme fashion   street fashion
> unfashionable   old-fashioned

b With your partner ask and answer the following questions.

1 Which style do you think is the most attractive? Why?

2 Would you be happy to wear any of these clothes? Which ones?

c Now use these words to describe the people in the pictures.

> cool   sporty   scruffy   smart
> well-dressed   casual   fashionable

d Use the verbs below to complete the sentences.

> fit   match   suit   go with

1 That style really .... her, she always looks really good.

2 The jacket doesn't .... her, it's much too tight!

3 Those trousers he's wearing .... his jacket, in fact it's a suit.

4 Those brown shoes don't .... a T-shirt and shorts. Trainers are better.

Listening

2a Imagine you have been invited to a friend's wedding. Talk to your partner about what you would wear.

1 Would you wear something fashionable /smart/unusual/casual/formal?

2 Would you wear a suit/a dress/a T-shirt and jeans?

b (16) Now listen to this conversation between Patricia and her boyfriend. Who knows most about what to wear – Patricia or Peter?

c (16) Listen again to the conversation. What does Patricia tell Peter to wear? Write Y (yes), N (no) and M (maybe) next to each photo.

d Look at the vocabulary in exercise 1c) again. Talk about these questions with a partner and try to use some of that vocabulary.

1 Ask your partner what plans she/he has for the weekend.

2 Ask him/her what he/she plans to wear.

3 Give your partner your opinions about their choice of clothes.

Phonology

▉ Sentence stress to clarify meaning

3a (17) Listen to this sentence pronounced in two different ways. Which word, or words, is stressed in each sentence?

1 Would you like to try the jacket with a matching skirt, or a dress?

2 Would you like to try the jacket with a matching skirt or a dress?

(17) Now listen to the two versions of the sentences again and repeat the stress patterns.

b (18) Now listen to these sentences and underline the stressed words. Tick the two options the shop assistant gives in each case.

1   Would you like to try the shirt with a tie, or a smart pullover?

   A ☐ a shirt and a tie

   B ☐ a pullover

   C ☐ a shirt and a pullover

2   Would you like to try the long-sleeved shirt or T-shirt?

   A ☐ a long-sleeved shirt

   B ☐ a short-sleeved T-shirt

   C ☐ a long-sleeved T-shirt

c (18) Now listen again and repeat.

Vocabulary

Money

4a Match the words (A-D) with their correct definitions (1-4).

   A ☐ a cheque   **C** ☐ debit card

   B ☐ credit card   **D** ☐ cash

1   you buy things with this small piece of plastic and pay for them the following month

2   your bank gives you these pieces of paper, which you can use to pay for things

3   real money – coins and notes

4   you get money from a machine and pay for things in shops with this small piece of plastic

b Work with a partner. Talk about these questions.

1   Which of these types of payment are common in your country?

2   Which one do you think is the most common?

3   Which type of payment do you usually use:

   A ☐ in a shop?

   B ☐ in a restaurant?

   C ☐ on the Internet?

4   Are there any places where credit and debit cards are not accepted in your country?

5a How do you think European families spend their money in these five countries? In small groups, try to answer the questions below.

1   Where do you think people spend most on food?

2   Where do people spend least on education?

3   Which do you think are the top and bottom countries for spending on health?

4   Which country spends most on entertainment?

When you have guessed the right answers, go to page 92 and check if you were right.

Grammar focus

Past Continuous

subject + *was/were* + verb + *-ing*
They **were talking** about the wedding.

We use the Past Continuous...

1 to describe past actions over a period of time.

It was the day before the party. Francesca and Simon **were making** *a cake and Isobel* **was trying** *to decide what to wear.*

What **were** *you* **doing** *last Friday?*

2 with the Past Simple to describe interrupted actions.

He **was shopping** *for a new suit when he* **realised** *that he didn't have his credit card.*

She **was wearing** *shorts and a T-shirt when it* **started** *raining.*

6a Complete these sentences using the Past Continuous form of a verb from the box.

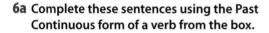

> work   eat   run   look   stay   talk

1   She .... to her friends about the party.

2   Steve .... his lunch when the phone rang.

3   .... (you) on the same project last year?

4   They .... in a cottage in France.

5   .... (Tom) when he fell over?

6   Daniel's family .... for a new house last year.

b Make sentences using the Past Continuous and Past Simple.

1   They/walk in park/dog escape

2   Megan/eat a sweet/tooth fall out

3   Mum/buy a new dress/see thief

4   Peter/phone ring/read newspaper

5   It/rain heavily/lights go out

6   We/shop online/steal credit card details

7   Now complete the gaps in this story with verbs in the Past Continuous or the Past Simple.

Last Saturday my friend Sarah and I ¹.................. shopping in the city centre. It was Juan's party that evening and we wanted to get something new to wear. We met at the bus stop at 10 o'clock but whilst we ².................. for the bus it ³.................. raining and we didn't have an umbrella. We took the bus into the centre but we ⁴.................. so much that we ⁵.................. our stop and had to get off at the next one. We finally got to our favourite shop and Sarah ⁶.................. the perfect dress for the party whilst I ⁷.................. for a new jumper. She was so pleased... until she ⁸.................. she didn't have her purse!

UNIT 5

Reading

8a Talk about these questions with another student.

1 What does *to tip* mean?

2 Have you ever worked in a place where you got tips? How did it make you feel?

3 Do you like giving tips? Are you generous or mean?

b Read the article below and find the words in the text that have these meanings:

1 impolite

2 the money you get paid each week for working

3 the piece of paper which tells you how much your meal has cost

4 well decorated and probably expensive

ADVICE ABOUT TIPPING IN ENGLAND

An American couple were eating dinner in a traditional pub restaurant during their trip to Britain last summer. As they were studying their bill at the end of the meal, they turned to a Britishman at the next table and asked him how much they should tip. He was confused and said, 'What tip?'. The American couple were looking at the man with surprise as they answered him, 'Well, some money for the waiter. Wouldn't it be rude not to leave a tip?'

Depending on where you are in the world, the unwritten 'rules' about tipping can be quite different. In America, for example, tips are considered to be compulsory, given that workers such as waiters, hairdressers and bar staff don't have very high wages. It is normal to add a 15% tip to the bill, or more if the service is particularly good.

In Britain tipping is more of a choice, depending on the kind of restaurant you are in and the quality of the service you receive. In an elegant restaurant a 10% tip is common, but if the service isn't good, then people generally won't leave a tip.

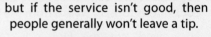

c Look at the article carefully again and decide whether the following statements are true (T) or false (F).

1 ☐ Americans and British people feel the same way about tipping.

2 ☐ In Britain you must give tips in cheap cafès.

3 ☐ Some Americans might be too generous.

4 ☐ British people give tips even when the service is not good.

d Speak to your partner about the following topics:

1 In your country, who do you tip? e.g. hairdressers? waiters? taxi-drivers? ......

2 How much do you normally tip? e.g. 5%? 10%? it depends on...?

3 Are there people in your country that you don't tip – even though they get tips in other countries?

Writing

ISE Reading into Writing

➡ *See Writing files on pages 78-91.*

9 Read the text again and then, in your own words, write a short article (approximately 150 words) for your school magazine:

i) telling the reader about tipping in the United Kingdom **and**

ii) saying what you think about tipping.

exam expert

Conversation phase

■ Preparing questions for the interview

Remember, in GESE and ISE examinations you have to talk **with** the examiner. This means that you have to answer the examiner's questions but you also have to **ask** some questions.

10 Complete the information about the Conversation phase using the words in the box.

examiner   one   all   portfolio   two

In the Conversation phase of the Grade 6 exam you will have to speak about ¹.............. of the subject areas from the syllabus. The ².............. will choose which ones to talk about, so you need to be prepared to talk about ³.............. of them. You must ask the examiner at least ⁴.............. question about each subject area.

The Conversation phase of the ISE I exam is divided into the following two parts:

1) discussion of your ⁵..............

2) discussion of a subject area chosen by the examiner.

You must ask the examiner one question in each part.

'Echo' questions

During natural conversations we often follow a pattern like this:

> **Question**
> **Examiner**: *Have you ever visited another country?*

> **Answer + 'echo' question**
> **Candidate**: *Yes, I've been to Canada. How about you? Do you travel much?*

> **Answer to 'echo' question**
> **Examiner**: *Yes, I do. I'm hardly ever at home!*

NB 'Echo' questions are about the same subject as the original question, but usually use different words.

11a Look at these other examples and complete the 'echo' question.

Conversation 1

Examiner: Are you interested in fashion?

Candidate: Well. not really, but my girlfriend loves fashionable clothes. How about you? ....?

Examiner: I'm more like you than like your girlfriend, I think!

Conversation 2

Examiner: Have you seen any good films lately?

Candidate: Yes. I've just seen *Harry Potter and the Deathly Hallows*. It was great! ....?

Examiner: Unfortunately, I just don't have enough time!

b Work with a partner. Take it in turns to be examiner and candidate and make short dialogues like these examples. Here are the questions for the 'examiners'.

1 Do you prefer travelling by train or plane?
2 When you travel do you like to use cash or a credit card?
3 Have you ever been to see an opera?
4 Have you been to a wedding or a birthday party recently?

Writing

ISE Portfolio/CW

➡ *See Writing files on pages 78-91.*

12 Reorder the stages (A-H) in practicing writing tasks for the ISE I exam.

A ☐ Give your text to your teacher.

B ☐ Write a first draft.

C ☐ Write a plan for your text.

D ☐ Write a second draft.

E ☐ Refer to the Writing file for help with how to write the text type.

F ☐ Listen to what your partner says about how you can improve your text.

G ☐ Swap texts with a partner and suggest ways for your partner to improve her/his text.

H ☐ Refer to exercises in this unit for help with subject area vocabulary and grammar.

13 Choose one, or more, of these writing tasks.

Correspondence *(ISE I 2009 (adapted))*

It is your cousin's 18th birthday soon. Your friend Maria has asked you what you are planning to wear. Write an email to Maria explaining how your cousin is going to celebrate her birthday and what you are planning to wear. Write 70-80 words.

Factual writing *(ISE I 2009)*

Write an article for a teenage magazine saying what items of clothes will be fashionable for young people this year. Give your opinion on the new styles and say which ones you will buy if you can. Write 110-130 words.

Creative/descriptive writing *(ISE I 2007)*

Write a short story for a writing competition about an Irish boy who went to America and became a millionaire. Write 110-130 words.

Trinity TAKE AWAY

Examiner: If I go to a restaurant tonight, do I need to leave a tip? How much?
Candidate: It really depends on the service you get. If it's good, about 10% of the bill would be good. Do you normally give tips in England?

UNIT **6**

Travel

Vocabulary

1a Match the names (1-7) with the continents (A-G).

1 ☐ Africa
2 ☐ Antarctica
3 ☐ Asia
4 ☐ Australia
5 ☐ Europe
6 ☐ North America
7 ☐ South America

b (19) Listen to the names of the continents from a) and mark the stress.

E.g. *África*

c (19) Listen again and repeat.

2 Work with a partner. Look at the photos and say where you think the places are.

E.g. I think Picture 1 is in Asia. What do you think?

Focus	
To express an opinion, say:	
I think	*it/Picture 1/he etc.* ***'s/is...***
	they/the pictures etc. ***'re/are...***
To request an opinion, say:	
What do you think?	

3a Match the words (A-D) with their definitions (1-4).

A travel (verb) **C** trip (noun)

B journey (noun) **D** travelling (noun)

1 ☐ the action of going from one place to another

2 ☐ the activity of visiting different places

3 ☐ when you go from one place to another

4 ☐ when you go to a place, usually for a short time, and come back again

b Complete these sentences with travel words from a).

1 .... is a good way to meet new people.

2 I .... a lot for my job, so I prefer to stay at home in my free time.

3 I want to go .... around the world after I finish university.

4 My .... to school is very quick – I can walk there in five minutes.

5 Our .... to New York was great. We only had three days there, but we saw so much.

6 The .... from London to Paris by train takes less than two and a half hours.

4a Work with a partner. Write the words and phrases from the box in the correct column.

> ~~the mountains~~ a lake backpacking
> camping ~~a cruise~~ by plane by boat/ferry
> self-catering (apartment, villa) a tent
> the countryside sunbathing ~~going sightseeing~~
> walking bed and breakfast (B&B)
> a package holiday relaxing ~~by train~~
> a city a beach holiday ~~a hotel~~ doing sport
> the seaside an activity holiday by car
> a youth hostel the desert

b Now look back at the photos on page 50 and, using words and phrases from a), say:

- what type of holiday is shown.
- what people do on this type of holiday.
- what type of accommodation people stay in.
- how people travel in this type of place.
- why people go to the type of place in the photos (see **Focus** box).

Focus
To express purpose, say:
I'm **going to** the beach **to relax**.
He **went** shopping **to buy** a new pair of shoes.
People **go to** Paris **to see** the famous sights.

holiday types	places	accommodation	activities	transport
a cruise	the mountains	a hotel	going sightseeing	by train

exam expert

Conversation phase

■ **Examiner and candidate roleplay**

5a Student A read the examiner rolecard and Student B read the candidate rolecard. Follow the instructions.

Student A: Examiner

Stage 1 Prepare questions to ask the candidate (Student B) about holidays:

- find out details about what she/he likes and doesn't like.

- use the categories in exercise 3a) when planning your questions.

Stage 2 Have the conversation with Student B.

Stage 3 Decide with Student B what went well in the conversation and what you could improve. Your teacher will also give you some ideas.

Student B: Candidate

Stage 1 The examiner (Student A) is going to ask you some questions about holidays. To prepare:

- think about the type of holidays you like and don't like and why.

- use the vocabulary in exercises 1, 2 and 3 when planning your answers.

Stage 2 Have the conversation with Student A.

Stage 3 Decide with Student A what went well in the conversation and what you could improve. Your teacher will also give you some ideas.

b Now change roles and repeat stages 1-3.

6a Read the blog posts (1-4) about holiday plans. What type of holiday does each person write about?

b Work with a partner. Tell each other which of the four trips you'd prefer to take and why.

c Underline phrases with the Present Continuous for future use and expressions relating to future time in the blog posts.

---

1 Louise, London, UK

At the end of July, I'm going on holiday for two weeks with some friends, to Spain. We're staying in an apartment at the seaside, on the Costa Brava, north of Barcelona. I can't wait!

---

2 Pierre, Bordeaux, France

I'm not really having a holiday this summer. I'm spending all of August studying English, in Brighton, on the south coast of England. I'm leaving on 31st July and coming back to France on 1st September. ☹

---

3 Jim, Seattle, USA

I'm going on a really cool trip in June. I'm going with my parents and my brother on a trip to Tanzania, in Africa, on a safari! It's going to be amazing!

---

4 Marina, Madrid, Spain

Well, I'm not really going on holiday this summer, but I am going away. I'm leaving at the beginning of August and coming back in a year's time! I'm going with a friend, and we're travelling around North and South America for a year, by train.

Grammar focus

Present Continuous for future use

To talk about fixed future plans, use:
am/are/is (not) + **verb** + **-ing** (Present Continuous) + **future time expression**.

At the end of July, I'**m going** on holiday for two weeks with some friends, to Spain.
I'**m not** really **having** a holiday **this summer**.
I'**m leaving at the beginning of August** and **coming back in a year's time**!
Are you **working the day after tomorrow**?

- When speaking, and in informal writing, we use the contractions '**m**/'**re**/'**s** instead of **am/are/is**.
- The future time expression can go at the beginning or end of the sentence.
- Sometimes the Present Continuous is used to talk about fixed future plans without the future time expression. This is because the time reference is implicit and/or has probably been mentioned already.

E.g. We'**re staying** in an apartment at the seaside...
I'**m going** with a friend...

7a Complete the sentences using information from the blog posts in exercise 6a).

1 Louise .... on holiday for two weeks at .... She .... in an apartment on the Costa Brava.

2 Pierre .... a real holiday this .... He .... all of .... studying English. He .... France on 31st July.

3 Jim .... on a trip to Africa with his parents, in ....

4 Marina .... at the .... August. She .... with a friend around North and South America for a year.

b Work with a partner. Ask and answer questions about future plans.

Questions	
Are you doing anything	next weekend?
What are you doing	next summer?
	on Saturday evening?
	the day after tomorrow?
	in a year's time?
	at Christmas? etc.

Answers
I'm playing in a basketball match next weekend.
No, I'm not doing anything. I haven't got any plans.

Follow-up questions
What about you?
And you? Are you doing anything on/at/in/for...?

c Now change partners. Tell your new partner about three of your previous partner's future plans.

UNIT 6

Reading

8a Work with a partner. Look at the photos and answer the questions.

1 What type of holiday do the photos show?
2 Would you like to go on a holiday like this? Why/Why not?

b With your partner, make a list of ways in which tourists on this type of holiday can save money on eating, travel and sightseeing.

E.g. **0** *Buy a young person's travelcard.*

TRAVEL ON THE CHEAP

1 ¹........... with the local tourist office if there are any special visitors' cards that will save you entrance fees at museums and attractions. Also, ask when or if museums and galleries have free openings.

2 ²........... whenever possible instead of paying for buses or the underground, and ³........... the cost of public transport if choosing a hostel or B&B out of town.

3 ⁴........... a Travelcard for the buses/trams/ underground if staying long enough to make it worthwhile (bring passport photos from home).

4 If you are staying in accommodation where breakfast is included, ⁵........... enough to keep

9a Read the advice from an article about how young travellers can save money. Match the paragraphs (1-6) to the categories (A-C).

A eating ..4.. ....
B travel ....
C sightseeing ......

b Now complete the article with the verbs from the box.

> buy   check (x2)   drink   eat (x2)   keep
> take (x2)   walk   waste

c Work with a partner. Read the article again and answer the questions.

1 Are any of the points in the article the same as the ones on your list in exercise 8b)?
2 Do you agree with all the advice for travellers in the article? Why/Why not?

you going for the day. This way, you can save money on lunch bills.

5 If you do get hungry during the middle of the day, set menus at lunchtime are far better value than dinner, so ⁶........... your main meal as a late lunch. And in Mediterranean countries, do as the locals do and ⁷........... your coffee at the bar – it costs a lot more to sit down.

6 If you are travelling by train or coach, ⁸........... a picnic with you. Don't ⁹........... valuable cash on expensive, poor quality railway or motorway service station food. ¹⁰........... a plastic water bottle and ¹¹........... re-filling it when you can.

Writing

ISE Reading into Writing

➡ *See Writing files on pages 78-91.*

10 Your English penfriend is coming on a backpacking holiday to your country. Using ideas from the text, write an email or letter to her/him (approximately 150 words):

i) explaining how she/he can save money on eating, travel and sightseeing in your country **and**

ii) inviting her/him to visit you.

Writing

ISE Portfolio/CW

➡ *See Writing files on pages 78-91.*

11 Choose one, or more, of these writing tasks. Follow the stages (A-H) to help you.

A Refer to the Writing File on pages 78-91 for help with how to write the text type.

B Refer to exercises in this unit for help with subject-area vocabulary and grammar.

C Write a plan for your text.

D Write a first draft.

E Swap texts with a partner and suggest ways for your partner to improve her/his text.

F Listen to what your partner says about how you can improve your text.

G Write a second draft.

H Give your text to your teacher.

Correspondence *(ISE I 2009)*

You have decided to live in America for a year. Write a letter to your penfriend giving your reasons for going there and telling him how you think the experience will help you. Ask your penfriend what he thinks about your plans. Write 70-80 words.

Factual writing *(ISE I 2010)*

Write an article for a travel magazine with the title, 'The importance of foreign travel'. Say why it is important to visit foreign countries, where you have been personally and what you learnt from the experience. Write 110-130 words.

Creative/descriptive writing *(ISE I 2010)*

Write a description for a website called www.terribletrips.com about the worst journey you have ever had. Describe the journey, say how long it took and explain why it was so bad. Write 110-130 words.

Topic phase

13a (20) Listen to Beatriz, a candidate from Spain, talking about her topic with the examiner. Number the points on her Topic form below in the order she mentions them.

b (20) Listen again and tick (✓) the extra questions that the examiner asks.

1. ☐ And who do you go with?
2. ☐ Have you got any friends there?
3. ☐ How long have your grandparents lived there?
4. ☐ So, when are you next going there?
5. ☐ What's it called again?
6. ☐ What's your favourite place in the village?

c (20) Listen again and underline the correct word or phrase.

0. Beatriz's favourite place is in the _mountains/city_.
1. The examiner has a problem understanding the _name/location_ of Beatriz's favourite place.
2. Beatriz goes to her favourite place _quite often/occasionally_.
3. Beatriz _always/sometimes_ goes to her favourite place alone.
4. Beatriz _always/doesn't always_ go there by train.
5. There are _more/fewer_ people in Beatriz's favourite place in the summer and at weekends.
6. You _can/can't_ ski in Cercedilla.
7. Beatriz doesn't like all the _rain/snow_ in Cercedilla.
8. Beatriz is going to Cercedilla _this/next_ month.

d (20) Listen to the last part of the recording again and complete the questions that Beatriz asks the examiner.

And .... you? ....
favourite place?

☐ How often I go there

☐ Location

☐ Things I don't like

My favourite place

☐ Why I like it

☐ What it's like

☐ Transport there

[0] Location

14 Complete the exam advice with the words *Do* or *Don't*.

Topic presentation – *Dos* and *Don'ts*

1 *Don't* choose a topic that you're not interested in or don't know much about.

2 .... prepare a monologue for the presentation. The examiner doesn't want you to just repeat a speech you've learnt.

3 .... expect to be asked about your topic in the order of the points on the Topic form.

4 .... complete the correct number of points on your Topic form – 6 for Grade 6 and ISE I.

5 .... prepare enough material to talk for up to five minutes.

6 .... ask the examiner at least one question on the subject of your topic.

7 .... bring pictures, photos, diagrams, models, maps, or other suitable objects to the exam, if you think they will help the discussion.

8 .... bring anything that's alive to the exam, e.g. insects or animals!

15a Student A read the examiner rolecard and Student B read the candidate rolecard. Follow the instructions.

Student A: Examiner

Stage 1 Prepare questions to ask the candidate (Student B) about a favourite place:

- Use the points for discussion from Beatriz's Topic form to help you think of things to ask.
- When Student B is ready, take her/his Topic form.

Stage 2 Ask Student B questions about the topic. Answer the question that she/he asks you.

Stage 3 Decide with Student B what went well in the presentation and what you could improve. Your teacher will also give you some ideas.

Student B: Candidate

Stage 1 Prepare a topic presentation about your favourite place.

- Use the discussion points from Beatriz's Topic form to help you think of what to say.
- Prepare your own Topic form with the same points.
- Give your Topic form to Student A.

Stage 2 Talk about your topic with Student A. Remember to ask the examiner a question.

Stage 3 Decide with Student A what went well in the presentation and what you could improve. Your teacher will also give you some ideas.

b Now change roles and repeat stages 1-3.

Trinity TAKE AWAY

Examiner: What type of holidays do you like best?
Candidate: I like lots of different types of holidays, but my favourite type is at the beach. One type of holiday I don't like is camping! This summer I'm going to the seaside in Spain – we're staying in a hotel.

UNIT **7**

Learning a language; Rules & regulations

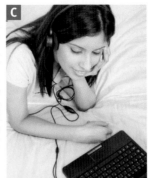

Vocabulary

▥ Learning a language

1a Match the photos (A-H) showing different ways of learning a foreign language with the phrases (1-8).

1 ☐ reading books, newspapers and magazines

2 ☐ listening to/watching things on the Internet

3 ☐ going to classes

4 ☐ having private lessons

5 ☐ studying with friends outside of class

6 ☐ living and working in a country where the language is spoken

7 ☐ learning lots of grammar and vocabulary

8 ☐ studying at school in the foreign language

b Work with a partner. Ask and answer the questions.

1 Which do you think are the three best ways in exercise 1a) to learn a language? Give reasons.

2 Which of these ways of learning a language have you tried? Which do you want to try in the future?

E.g. I think having private lessons is a good way to learn a language, because the teacher can give you lots of attention.

I want to live in Australia when I'm older, to learn English there.

Reading

2a Read the tips from an article about language learning and match the headings (A-D) with the paragraphs (1-4).

A Errors

B Listening

C Reading

D Understanding

b Work with a partner. Ask and answer these questions.

1 Which do you think is the most useful tip? Give reasons.

2 Which do you think is the most difficult tip to follow? Give reasons.

E.g. I think the tip about errors is really useful. I worry too much about making mistakes!

3 Match the phrases in bold (1-9) in the text in exercise 2a) with their function (A-D).

A It's necessary to do ....

B It's not necessary to do ....

C It's necessary **not** to do ....

D It's possible, but not certain ...2... ....

Learning a Language

Are you studying hard, but not making much progress? Are you thinking: 1 *What do I have to do to really learn a language?* Follow these tips to find out.

1 ☐ You won't understand everything – in fact, at the beginning of the learning process, 2 **you might not understand much at all**. But 3 **you need to accept** that 4 **you don't have to understand everything** to be able to communicate.

2 ☐ To learn a language, you have to practise it. This means 5 **you have to speak** – and sometimes to write. And when you're speaking and writing you will make mistakes, but 6 **you mustn't get demotivated** by this. Instead, learn from the mistake you make – how can I say that correctly? – and 7 **next time, you might get it right!**

3 ☐ This is an essential aspect of learning a language – 8 **you need to hear other people speaking it to be able to speak it yourself**. You can get lots of material from the Internet – videos, podcasts, news broadcasts. Put it on your MP3 player and practise this skill wherever you go.

4 ☐ This really helps with learning a foreign language, but 9 **you must choose things that you're interested in**. So, if you love photography, get a magazine about photography, or print out an article about it from the Internet in the language you're trying to learn.

Grammar focus

Expressing obligation, necessity and uncertainty

1 To express obligation and necessity, use *must*, *have to* and *need to* + infinitive.
*...you **need to hear** other people speaking.*
*...you **have to speak**.*
*...you **must choose** things that you're interested in.*

2 To express lack of obligation, use *don't* (*do not*)/*doesn't* (*does not*) *have to* + infinitive.
*...you **don't have to understand** everything to be able to communicate.*

3 To express negative obligation, use *musn't* (*must not*) + infinitive.
*...you **mustn't get** demotivated by this.*

4 To express uncertainty, use: *might/might not* + infinitive.
*...you **might not understand** much at all.*

5 To ask questions about obligation or rules, use *do/does* + subject + *have to* + infinitive.
*What **do I have to do** to really learn a language?*

4a Complete the sentences with language to express obligation, necessity and uncertainty from the box.

1 I .... do two hours' homework every afternoon – it's too much!

2 You .... revise for your English exam – you failed your last one!

3 We .... go to London for New Year, but we're not sure – my Mum doesn't know if she .... work or not.

4 You .... play music after 11p.m., because I can't sleep if there's noise.

5 He .... study very hard, he passes his exams them easily without studying!

6 What time .... start school in the morning?

7 I speak some Spanish, but I'm worried that I .... understand anything when I go to Peru on holiday.

8 .... study a lot to learn Chinese?

b Work with a partner to answer these questions about your native language/s.

1 Do many people from other countries speak your language? Do some nationalities tend to speak your language better than others? Why do you think this is?

2 What aspects of your language are easy to learn?

3 What aspects of your language are difficult to learn?

4 Make a list of what someone has to do to really learn your language well.

E.g.

Valeria, Italy
'It's easy to learn to read Italian, because there are clear rules for how to pronounce the letters. Not like in English!'

Anthi, Greece
'Having to learn a different alphabet can make Greek difficult for people to learn.'

c Change partners and compare your lists from exercise 4b) question 4.

Phonology

■ Connected speech at sentence level: stress and weak forms

4a (21) Listen to these sentences from the article on page 59 and mark the stress in each one.

0 You might not understand much at all.
1 You don't have to understand everything.
2 You mustn't get demotivated.
3 You need to hear other people speaking.
4 You must choose things that you're interested in.
5 What do I have to do to really learn a language?

b (21) Listen and repeat the sentences from a).

c (22) Listen to some more sentences and write in the box the number of words that you hear. Contractions count as two words.

1 ☐ ....
2 ☐ ....
3 ☐ ....
4 ☐ ....
5 ☐ ....

d (22) Listen again and write the sentences you hear.

e (22) Listen and repeat the sentences from d).

Vocabulary

■ Rules and regulations

6a Work with a partner and answer these questions.

1 What do the signs (1-14) below show that you musn't do?
2 Where would you see these signs?
3 Do you agree that it's a good idea to stop people doing these things? Give reasons.

E.g. Number 1 shows that you musn't take photos. You might see this in an art gallery.

Yes, I think it's a good idea to stop people doing this, because the camera flash can damage the paintings.

b Make a list in the table of the rules and regulations in your life.

at home:
I have to make my bed in the mornings.
at school/work:
I have to wear a uniform to school.
in the public places I go to:
I have to wear a hat in the swimming pool.

c Work with a partner. Using your list from b), to ask and answer questions about the rules and regulations in your life, at home, at school/work and in public places. Say how you feel about each one.

E.g. **A:** Do you have to make your own bed?

B: No, my Dad does it for me! I'm lucky.

A: Do you have to wear a school uniform?

B: Yes, and I hate it!

7 Work in groups of three or four and follow these instructions.

1 Talk about the schools you go to, or went to in the past, the rules and regulations that they have/had and how you would like to change them.

2 Write a list of rules for a perfect school.

3 Present your rules to the class.

4 Vote to decide which group has the most perfect school.

Writing

ISE Reading into Writing

8a Complete the text about strange laws around the world with the countries in the box.

> *Arkansas, USA   Athens, Greece   Britain (x4)*
> *Florida, USA   France   Miami, USA*
> *Singapore   Vermont, USA*

b Now, go to page 92 and check your answers.

c Work with a partner. Ask and answer these questions.

1 Which do you think is the strangest law above?

2 Which is the least strange law?

3 What reasons could there be behind each law?

E.g. I think they're all very stange, but, for me, the one about the whale is the strangest!

Does it feel like your life is full of rules? That people are telling you what to do at home, at school, in the street – wherever you go? Well, if you think that there are too many rules where you live, check out these weird and wonderful laws from around the world.

1 In ...., it's illegal to skateboard in a police station.

2 In ...., it's illegal to chew chewing gum.

3 It's illegal to die in the Houses of Parliament in ....

4 In ...., it's illegal to put a stamp with the head of the British queen upside down on a letter.

5 In ...., you can't call a pig Napoleon.

6 In ...., unmarried women who parachute on Sundays can be put in prison.

7 In ...., women must get written permission from their husbands to wear false teeth.

8 In .... if a dead whale is found on the coast, the head is legally the property of the king and the tail of the queen.

9 In ...., the police can take your driving licence away if they think your are badly dressed or aren't clean.

10 In ...., it's illegal for a woman getting married for the second time to wear a white wedding dress.

11 In ...., all swans are owned by the queen and it's illegal to hunt them.

➡ *See Writing files on pages 78-91.*

9 **Using ideas from the text on page 62, in your own words, write an article (approximately 150 words) for your school online magazine:**

i) giving examples of the strange laws in different countries, including examples from your own country if you know any **and**

ii) saying what you think are the reasons behind the laws **and**

iii) describing a law in your country that you think needs to change.

exam expert

Conversation phase

■ **Talking about your portfolio**

10a (23) **Listen to Rosa, an ISE candidate, talking to the examiner about her Portfolio, and answer the questions.**

1 How many questions does the examiner ask Rosa about the **content** of the tasks?

2 How many questions does the examiner ask her about **how** she wrote the tasks?

b (23) **Listen again and say if these statements are true (T) or false (F).**

1 ☐ Rosa doesn't want to be a travel writer.

2 ☐ Rosa has got strong ideas about things that are wrong with schools.

3 ☐ Rosa did three drafts of the tasks and then the final version.

4 ☐ Rosa's teacher was the only person who helped her improve her tasks.

5 ☐ Rosa doesn't know exactly how long it took her to write the tasks.

c (23) **Use the phrases in the box to complete Rosa's answers.**

> *for each task   I'd say   I'm not really sure*
> *It's difficult to say   Maybe about*
> *my teacher gave me advice   I thought that*
> *Well, mainly because*

Examiner A: Why did you choose this question?
Rosa: ¹ .... I may really want to write to an English-speaking friend about this one day.

Examiner B: Why did you choose to write a description of the perfect school for the future?
Rosa: ² .... I've got strong opinions about how I'd like school to be.

Examiner C: Now, which task did you enjoy doing the most?
Rosa: ³ .... the description of the perfect school.

Examiner D: Tell me, how many drafts did you do for the tasks, before the final version?
Rosa: I did two drafts ⁴ ....

Examiner E: Did anyone help you improve the first two drafts?
Rosa: Yes, some other students in my class suggested ways to improve the first draft, then ⁵ .... about the second draft.

Examiner F: So how long did it take you to do the tasks?
Rosa: ⁶ .... exactly... ⁷ .... five hours in total for each task – ⁸ ....

d **Underline the language in the questions and answers in exercise 10d) that will be useful for talking about your portfolio, then compare with a partner.**

11 Complete the exam advice with the words in the box.

> content   difficult   enjoyed   who   long
> many   why   question

TALKING ABOUT YOUR PORTFOLIO

You might have to:

1 talk about .... you chose the tasks.

2 give more information and/or details about the .... of the tasks.

3 tell the examiner how .... drafts you wrote.

4 say how .... it took you to write the tasks.

5 talk about .... helped you improve the tasks.

6 say which task was the easiest/most .... one for you.

7 say which task you .... doing the most.

And remember:

8 you have to ask the examiner a .... about the content of your portfolio text.

12a Student A is the examiner, Student B is the candidate. Follow the instructions on the rolecards below.

b Change roles and repeat stages 1-4.

Student A: Examiner

Stage 1 The candidate will give you a piece of portfolio writing.

Stage 2 Plan questions to ask the candidate about the content of the text and how she/he wrote it.

- Refer back to the language you underlined in the questions in exercise 10d).

Stage 3 Have a conversation about the piece of writing with the candidate.

Stage 4 Decide with Student B what went well in the conversation and what you could improve. Your teacher will also give you some ideas.

Student B: Candidate

Stage 1 Give the examiner a piece of your portfolio writing.

Stage 2 Think about the questions that the examiner might ask you about the content of your text and how you wrote it and plan your answers.

- Refer back to the language you underlined in the answers in exercise 10d).

- Plan a question to ask the examiner about the content of your text.

Stage 3 Have a conversation with the examiner about your piece of writing. Remember to ask the examiner a question about the content of your text.

Stage 4 Decide with Student A what went well in the conversation and what you could improve. Your teacher will also give you some ideas.

Writing

ISE Portfolio/CW

➡ *See Writing file on pages xx.*

13 **Choose one, or more, of these writing tasks. Follow the stages (A-H) to help you.**

A Refer to the Writing file for help with how to write the text type.

B Refer to exercises in this unit for help with subject area vocabulary and grammar.

C Write a plan for your text.

D Write a first draft.

E Swap texts with a partner and suggest ways for your partner to improve her/his text.

F Listen to what your partner says about how you can improve your text.

G Write a second draft.

H Give your text to your teacher.

Factual writing *(ISE I 2010)*

Write an article for a family magazine about rules teenagers have to follow in your country. Describe two of these rules and give your opinion on them. Say what happens if someone breaks the rules. Write 110-130 words.

Creative/descriptive writing *(ISE I 2010)*

Write a story for a writing competition beginning with the words, 'There is one school rule I'll never break again...' Describe the rule, say how you broke it and explain why this had serious consequences. Write 110-130 words.

Correspondence *(ISE I 2008)*

Your English friend is planning to hire a car while on holiday in your country. Write an email to your friend saying what the most important driving rules are. Explain what will happen if he does not follow the rules. Write 110-130 words.

Trinity TAKE AWAY

Examiner: What do you **have to do** to learn a foreign language well?

Candidate: I think you **have to** listen a lot, and practise speaking as much as you can. You **mustn't** get demotivated when you make mistakes – they **might** help you to get it right next time!

UNIT 8

Health & fitness

How much do you know about health and fitness? Do this quiz to find out.

1 How many litres of water do you need to drink every day to keep healthy?

A a litre

B two litres

C half a litre

2 To stay fit, you need to exercise for at least

A 20 minutes two or three times a week.

B an hour two or three times a week.   C 10 minutes two or three times a week.

3 For a healthy diet, you need to eat fruit and/or vegetables at least

A twice a week.

B five times a day.

C once a day.

4 If you want to sleep well, don't drink coffee   A after 8 p.m.   B after 3 p.m.   C after midday.

5 You need to eat fish

A two or three times a month.

B five times a day.

C two or three times a week.

6 Which food has fat that is good for you?

A margarine

B extra virgin olive oil

C chips

7 To help solve a problem that's causing you stress,

A try to forget about it.   B take medicine for it.

C talk about it with people.

8 The biggest preventable cause of death and disease in the world is

A smoking.   B AIDS.   C stress.

Vocabulary

◼ Health and fitness 1

1a Circle the answers (A–C) you think are correct in the quiz, then compare with a partner.

b (24) Listen to a radio presenter giving the answers to the quiz questions and tick (✓) the correct answers.

c (24) Listen again and match the phrase/s (A–H) with the quiz questions on page 66.

A	☐	10 million deaths
B	☐	wait for 24 hours
C	☐	having more energy
D	☐	stopping depression
E	☐ 1	keeping your heart healthy
F	☐	preventing some cancers
G	☐	something not to do after lunch
H	☐	vitamins and minerals your body needs

d Now tell a partner:

- how many of your answers from a) are correct.
- if there are any facts or statistics in the quiz that surprised you.
- which of the things in the quiz you do to keep healthy – or don't do!

Focus

To express surprise, you can say:

That	
It	***was a surprise** to me.*
etc.	
*I **was surprised** about*	*this.*
	that.
	etc.

E.g. I was surprised about the answer to question 1 – I never drink that much water in a day.

The answer to question 4 was a surprise to me – I always have a coffee before I go to bed.

e (25) Complete the sentences from the recording in exercise 1, then listen again to check. Compare your answers with a partner.

1 If you .... to be healthy, you .... to drink at least two litres of water per day...

2 If you .... more water, you .... less chance of getting heart disease...

3 ...if you .... caffeine in the afternoon, it .... stop you sleeping at night.

4 ...when you .... about the problem to someone, you .... better...

Grammar focus

Zero conditional

To express certainty about the consequences of a situation; to talk about a fact – something that is always true, use:

if/when + present verb form   present verb form
If you **want** *to be healthy, you* **need** *to drink at least two litres of water per day.*

First conditional

To express certainty and possibility about the consequences of a present or future situation, use:

if/when + present verb form   *will/will not* (or *may/may not*) + infinitive
If you **drink** *more water, you'***ll have** *less chance of getting heart disease.*
If you **drink** *caffeine in the afternoon, it* **may stop** *you sleeping at night.*

If you're sure about the consequence, use **will/won't**.
If you're not so sure, use **may/may not**.

When speaking, and in informal writing, we use these contractions:
- *'ll = will*
- *won't = will not*

The clause with *'ll/won't* (or **may**) + infinitive can also go first, with *if* + present verb form as the second clause.

2a Complete the conditional sentences using the words in brackets.

0 If people ..*eat*.. (*eat*) lots of fast food, it...*'s*.... (*be*) bad for their health.

1 If she .... (*talk*) to someone about her problems, I'm sure she .... (*feel*) better.

2 You .... (*not sleep*) very well tonight if you .... (*have*) a cup of coffee now. It's 9 p.m.

3 If you .... (*drink*) lots of water, you .... (*have*) less chance of getting some cancers.

4 If he .... (*eat*) chips every day, he .... (put on) weight. It's very simple!

5 When people .... (*eat*) less and .... (*do*) exercise, they .... (*lose*) weight.

6 They eat a lot of butter. If they .... (*use*) extra virgin olive oil instead, they .... (*be*) healthier.

7 We .... (*not go*) to the party if we .... (*not find*) a babysitter.

8 When she .... (*come*) back from her holiday, she .... (*phone*) me, I'm sure.

b Work in pairs. Write a list of ten points on how people can be healthier and fitter. Use information from the previous two pages and ideas of your own.

E.g. If you exercise twice a week, for at least twenty minutes, you'll be fitter.

c Compare your list with another pair's. Are any of your points the same?

Phonology

■ Intonation at sentence level

3a (26) **Listen to a fitness instructor giving advice about keeping fit. As you listen to the advice, complete the information below.**

1 It helps if ....

2 If you don't have a good diet, ...

3 If you do some exercise, ...

4 When you exercise, ...

5 You'll have less chance of getting heart disease if ....

6 If you exercise twice a week, ...

7 It'll be more fun ....

8 If you want to stay healthy, ...

b **What do you notice about the instructor's voice at the end of each sentence?**

c (26) **Now listen again and repeat the sentences.**

Vocabulary

■ Health and fitness 2

4a **Match the healthcare words in the box with the people and places in the photos (A-F).**

1 chemist's/pharmacy   4 optician
2 dentist   5 physiotherapist
3 nurse   6 surgery

b (27) **Listen and repeat the words from a).**

c **Now use the words to complete the sentences.**

1 I think I need stronger glasses. I'll make an appointment with the .... for an eye test next week.

2 My tooth hurts. I need to see a ....

3 The person that a doctor treats is called a ....

4 I've hurt my back – I think I need some sessions with a .... to make it better.

5 The .... is closed at weekends – if you need to see a doctor then, you have to go to the hospital.

6 My stay in hospital wasn't too bad – one very kind .... even brought me a cup of tea in the middle of the night!

7 When you go to the ...., can you buy me some aspirin?

8 I don't think you need to see a doctor – you can ask the .... to suggest some medicine to buy.

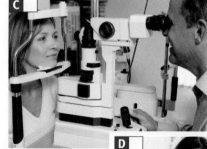

C

A

B

D

E

F

UNIT 8

Reading

5a Which healthcare services are free in your country? Which do you pay for? With a partner, make a list:

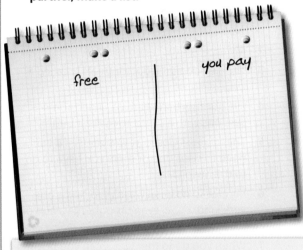

free | you pay

b Read the information about some of the healthcare services that are available free in Britain with the National Health Service (NHS). Are they the same as your list of free services in a)?

c Read the information again and match the headings (A-D) to the paragraphs (1-4).

  A NHS Direct online

  B NHS walk-in centres

  C Dental access centres

  D GP surgeries

ACCESSIBLE HEALTHCARE

1 ☐ These centres provide a complete range of NHS dental services, including routine as well as urgent care. People do not need to register to see a dentist in an access centre and the centres are open at times when patients can get to them.

2 ☐ The first point of contact for many people when they develop a health problem is their local doctor, also known as a general practitioner (GP). These doctors usually form a small practice, or surgery, to serve a particular neighbourhood. GPs look after the health of people in their local community and deal with a whole range of health problems.

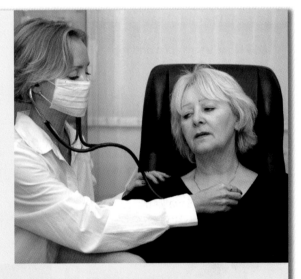

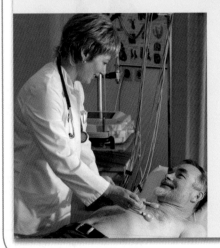

3 ☐ These centres offer fast access to health advice and treatment. They are open and available to anyone and provide:

- a seven days a week service, from early in the morning until late in the evening.
- assessment by an experienced NHS nurse.
- treatment for minor injuries and illnesses.
- advice on how to stay healthy.
- information on local services.

4 ☐ This is the gateway to health advice and information on the Internet. It includes an easy-to-use guide to treating common symptoms at home and links to thousands of sources of help and advice.

Writing

ISE Reading into Writing

➡ *See Writing file on pages 78-91.*

6 Now write a report (approximately 150 words) for a health magazine about the free healthcare services that are available in Britain and in your country. Say which are most useful for patients and why.

Phonology

■ Intonation patterns of more complex question forms

7a (28) Listen to the questions and draw arrows where the voice goes up and down.

0 What do you think about getting healthcare advice on the Internet?

1 Have you ever been to a hospital? If so, was it to visit someone or because you were ill?

2 When did you last visit your GP? What was wrong with you?

3 What are the opening times of your local surgery? What happens if you're ill when it's closed?

4 How often do you go to the dentist's? How do you feel about going?

b (28) Listen again and repeat the questions.

c Work with a partner. Ask and answer the questions in a).

d Are these statements true (T) or false (F), according to the text?

1 ☐ Dental access centres only provide a service for emergencies.

2 ☐ Dental access centres are only open during normal working hours, e.g. 9 a.m.-5 p.m.

3 ☐ A GP is another name for a local doctor.

4 ☐ GPs look after people in a specific area.

5 ☐ Anyone can go to an NHS walk-in centre.

6 ☐ You can see a doctor at an NHS walk-in centre.

7 ☐ At NHS walk-in centres, you can find out lots of information about health.

8 ☐ NHS Direct online gives advice to help people treat minor illnesses themselves.

EMERGENCY

→ Emergency Patient Parking

↑ Main Entrance

→ Physician

exam expert

Conversation phase

■ Health and fitness

9a Work with a partner and follow these instructions.

1 Make a list of the different areas of health and fitness the examiner may ask you about in the Conversation phase. Refer to exercises 1, 4 and 5 for help.

   E.g. *keeping fit*

2 Now prepare some questions for the examiner to ask about each of the areas on your list and think about how the candidate could answer the questions.

   How many times a week do you exercise?
   Once or twice.
   What do you do to keep fit?
   I go swimming and I play tennis.

3 Prepare two questions that the candidate could ask the examiner about health and fitness.

b One of you is Student A, the other Student B. Student A read the examiner rolecard and Student B read the candidate rolecard. Follow the instructions.

c Now change roles and repeat stages 1-2.

Student A: Examiner

Stage 1 Have a conversation with the candidate (Student B) about health and fitness. Use the questions you prepared above. Answer the question/s that the candidate asks you.

Stage 2 Decide with Student B what went well in the conversation and what you could improve. Your teacher will also give you some ideas.

Student B: Candidate

Stage 1 Have a conversation with the examiner (Student A) about health and fitness. Remember to ask the examiner at least one question.

Stage 2 Decide with Student A what went well in the conversation and what you could improve. Your teacher will also give you some ideas.

Topic phase

■ Choosing a topic

10a Work with a partner. Make a list of 10 possible topics to talk about in the Topic phase.

- My favourite sport

- My hero

b Compare your list with another pair. Add any of their topics that you haven't got on your list.

c Choose the topic from your list that you are most interested in.

72

d Ask your partner these questions.

1 What topic did you choose in c)?

2 Are you really interested in this topic?

3 Can you say something about this topic in your own language?

4 Do you know any vocabulary for this topic already in English?

5 Will you feel comfortable talking about this topic in English?

6 Do you want to know more about this topic?

7 Will you feel confident answering questions about this topic?

8 Is there enough to say about this topic to speak for five minutes?

e If you answered 'yes' to questions 2-8 in d), then it is a good topic for you to choose. If not, look back at your list in b) and choose another one.

f With the topic you have chosen in c) or e), plan three things to say about it now. Ask your teacher for any vocabulary you need.

g Work with a partner. Take it in turns to present the three points you planned in f) about your topic. Ask your partner at least three questions about the points they make.

Writing

ISE Portfolio/CW

➡ *See Writing file on pages 78-91.*

11 Choose one, or more, of these questions.

Correspondence *(ISE I 2010)*

You have recently become very fit. Write an email to a friend saying what you have done to reach your new level of fitness and explaining what you were doing wrong before you became fit. Invite your friend to exercise with you. Write 70-80 words.

Factual writing *(ISE I 2010)*

A fast food restaurant has just opened in your area. Write a report for a healthy-eating organisation explaining what food the restaurant serves and why it is unhealthy. Say what health problems people might have if they eat a lot of fast food. Write 110-130 words.

Creative/descriptive writing

Write the diary of a famous sportsperson on a day when she/he is training hard to get fit. Give details about exercise and food. Write 110-130 words.

Trinity TAKE AWAY

Examiner: What do you think is the best way to have a healthy lifestyle?

Candidate: Well, it's really important to have a healthy diet, for example, to eat five portions of fruit and vegetables a day and to eat fish regularly too. If you do some exercise two or three times a week, you can keep fit too.

1 Circle the correct option in the sentences (1-8).

1 You can't go to the party in those clothes! You look really *smart/scruffy*!

2 Look at that jacket! It's so *cool/old-fashioned*! I love it, but it's too expensive!

3 Those trousers don't *suit/fit* you anymore – I think you've grown!

4 That dress really *suits/matches* you – it's exactly the same colour as your eyes.

5 My grandmother always tries to pay *by cheque/in cash*, but they don't accept them in lots of places nowadays.

6 I like going *on package holidays/backpacking* – I don't have to make any plans myself, it's all organised for me!

7 My brother always stays at *bed and breakfast places/youth hostels* when he's on holiday, because they're cheap.

8 My parents like staying in *hotels/self-catering accommodation* when we go away, so that they don't have to do any cooking!

2 Complete the sentences with the correct form of the verb in brackets, the Past Continuous or Past Simple.

1 I .... (*backpack*) in Turkey when I first .... (*meet*) my boyfriend.

2 It .... (*rain*), so we .... (*decide*) not to go for a walk.

3 I .... (*do*) my homework when they .... (*arrive*).

4 We .... (*shop*) for six hours, but .... (*not find*) the right dress for the wedding.

5 I .... (*get*) really fit last year – I .... (*exercise*) a lot and .... (*eat*) really well.

3 It's Sunday evening. Marina is talking on the phone to a friend about her plans for the next week. Look at her diary and write what she says about her plans for each day using the Present Continuous + future time reference.

Monday
8 a.m. university
6 p.m. English class
Tuesday

Wednesday
8 a.m. university
Thursday
11 a.m. yoga class
6 p.m. English class

Friday
11 a.m. university
Saturday
5 p.m. shopping with mum
8 p.m. cinema with Fabio
Sunday
visit grandma and grandpa

4 Complete the sentences (1-6) using *have to, must, don't have to, mustn't* and *might*.

1 Emilio's parents give him a lot of freedom – he .... be home by any particular time the evenings.

2 Poor Lucy. She .... be home by 10 p.m., even on Saturdays!

3 If you fail an exam, you .... give up. You just .... work harder the next time!

4 You .... find learning a another language hard when you first start.

5 You .... get depressed if you make mistakes – that's how you learn!

6 I .... wear a hat in the swimming pool and I hate it!

5 Find words about healthcare people and places in Unit 8 to match the definitions (1-5).

1 The place where you go to see your local doctor. ....

2 The person who looks after you in hospital. ....

3 If you need new glasses, you go to see this person. ....

4 The person that you buy medicine from. ....

5 There are two words for this place where you buy medicine. ....

6 Match the two halves (1-6 and A-F) of the following conditional sentences.

1 If you go into town this afternoon,
2 If we don't hurry up,
3 You may lose some weight,
4 He'll fail his exams,
5 If you want to be healthy,
6 If you're having a good time,

A ☐ if he doesn't study harder.
B ☐ I may come with you.
C ☐ if you eat less fatty food.
D ☐ we'll miss the train!
E ☐ you need to drink at least two litres of water per day.
F ☐ we'll stay for longer.

7

Con...
answers...

1 Are you inte...
2 Do you travel mu...
3 In the UK, do you norm...
4 Have you seen the new Harr...
5 When you travel, do you prefer to... or credit cards?
6 What do you do to keep fit?

A ☐ Not really, no, not now. But I was when I was younger.

B ☐ Yes, quite a lot, with my job. And then on holiday a couple of times a year.

C ☐ Yes, usually, unless you're really not happy with the service.

D ☐ Well, actually, I always take both with me, then I've always got a way of paying!

E ☐ Well, I go running about three times a week, and I do yoga whenever I can.

F ☐ Yes, I saw it last week. I thought it was great!

Grade 6 Self-evaluation

Write Y (yes) or N (needs more practice) for each statement.

1 ☐ I can talk about fashion.
2 ☐ I can talk about money.
3 ☐ I can talk about travel.
4 ☐ I can talk about learning a language.
5 ☐ I can talk about rules and regulation.
6 ☐ I can talk about health and fitness.
7 ☐ I can talk about future plans using the Present Continuous + future time expression.
8 ☐ I can use *have to*, *need to*, *must*, *don't have to*, *mustn't* and *might* accurately.
9 ☐ I can use the first conditional accurately.

...e prepared. The examiner will ask you
...ll choose points from your Topic form

...phase is:

...opic form, please?

...topic.

...phase for Grades 5 and 6

The exa... ...ct areas for the grade (see Overview, pages 4-5) and will
expect you to ... ...earn the vocabulary and prepare all six subject areas for
the grade. The follow... ...ples of possible examiner and candidate language for
each grade.

Match candidates' questions
...versation phase (1-6) with the
...(A-F).
...rom the
...examiner's
...ch?
...rested in fashion?
...Potter film?
...lly give tips?
...se cash

(30) Grade 5

Examiner: Which festivals are popular in your country?
Candidate: We celebrate many festivals, but I think the most important one is carnival, in February.

Examiner: Which is the best way to travel around your city?
Candidate: Well, the fastest means of transport is the underground, but the cheapest is the bus.

Examiner: Will you spend Christmas with your family this year?
Candidate: Yes, definitely. We always eat lunch with my aunt and uncle on 25th December.

Examiner: What was the last film you saw at the cinema?
Candidate: I saw the new Harry Potter film two weeks ago – it was excellent!

Examiner: Which do you prefer, hip hop or pop music?
Candidate: I prefer hip hop. What about you, do you like pop music?
Examiner: Yes, I do, but I prefer classical music!

Examiner: Have you done anything special recently?
Candidate: Yes, I went to Bilbao two weeks ago, because my cousin lives there.

Grade 6

Examiner: What were the tourists doing when the tour guide was speaking?
Candidate: Some were looking at the Eiffel Tower and others were taking photographs.

Examiner: Do you have to help your parents in the house?
Candidate: No, but if I don't, they don't give me any pocket money.

Examiner: If you go to the party on Saturday, what will you wear?
Candidate: I think I'll go shopping on Saturday to buy something new.

Examiner: What time does school start?
Candidate: Well, lessons start at 9 o'clock, but we have to be there at 8.50 for registration.

Examiner: Do you prefer playing sport or watching it?
Candidate: I prefer playing sport, but this weekend I'm watching Arsenal play against Liverpool.

Examiner: What is the best way to remember new vocabulary in English?
Candidate: If I write an example sentence using each word, it helps me to remember the vocabulary.

2b Focus on the Conversation phase for ISE I

The examiner will choose **one** of the **subject areas** for ISE I (see **Overview**, page 5) and will expect you to discuss it. You need to learn the vocabulary and prepare all six subject areas for the level. These are the same as those for Grade 6 (see examples above).

In ISE I, you also have to discuss your Portfolio work in the conversation. The following are some examples of possible examiner and candidate language during the discussion of the portfolio.

ISE I

Examiner: Why did you choose question number three in Section 1 – an email explaining why you have chosen to run a marathon?
Candidate: Well, I often go running so I knew what to write about.

Examiner: Why did you choose to write a description of your favourite film star in Section 3?
Candidate: Because I love going to the cinema and I think Daniel Radcliffe is great!

Examiner: Now, which task did you enjoy doing the most?
Candidate: Probably the report about teenagers and money.

Examiner: Why?
Candidate: Because I feel really strongly about this subject.

Examiner: How many drafts did you do for the tasks, before the final version?
Candidate: I did two drafts for each task.

Examiner: Did anyone help you improve the first two drafts?
Candidate: Yes, some other students in my class suggested ways to improve the first draft, then my teacher gave me advice about the second draft...

Examiner: How long did it take you to do the tasks?
Candidate: It's difficult to say exactly. Maybe about five hours in total for each task.

writing file

Correspondence – informal emails & letters

ISE I Controlled Written exam (approx. 150 words), Portfolio Section 1 (70-80 words)

1 **Read the task and the email that a candidate called Rosa writes for it.**

You are planning to spend six months travelling the world. Write an email to your English friend saying which countries you intend to visit and what you will see there. Invite your friend to come with you. (ISE I 2011)

To: Lucy@CIDEBmail.co.uk

Subject: News!

Hi Lucy,

How are you?

I've got some exciting news to tell you! I'm going on a trip around the world for six months with my friend Clara! We're flying to New York at the beginning of July and we're spending a week there sightseeing. Then we're getting the train to Washington because Clara really wants to see the White House.

After that, we're flying down to Mexico City and are planning to spend two months travelling around Latin America – seeing the Amazon River in Brazil is definitely on our list! We're not sure where we're going to go after that, but probably somewhere in Asia. We've got round-the-world plane tickets, so we can decide later.

Pretty cool, don't you think?! Why don't you come with us?

Love,

Rosa x

2 Using Rosa's email to help you, complete the information about informal emails and letters with words/phrases from the box.

> *after closing don't first name friend full forms future invite logically subject*

Purpose	<ul><li>to thank or ¹.................... someone</li><li>to give/ask for advice or to describe something</li><li>to give reasons for something</li><li>to tell someone about a past or ².................... event</li></ul>	
Typical readers	<ul><li>a ³.................... /penfriend</li><li>a member of your family</li></ul>	
Organisation and layout	**Emails**	**Letters**
	<ul><li>Write on email software and print out.</li><li>Date can be in your own language (it is generated automatically).</li><li>Complete the ⁴.................... line (not included in word count).</li></ul>	<ul><li>Sender's address optional (not included in word count); **don't** include recipient's address.</li><li>Date is optional (not included in word count). If included, it goes above the greeting.</li></ul>
	<ul><li>Organise the information you need to include ⁵...................., in paragraphs.</li></ul>	
Features	<ul><li>Language style is informal.</li><li>Language structures and functions depend on purpose of email/letter, e.g. Present Continuous for future use to tell someone about a future event.</li><li>Use correct spelling and punctuation; ⁶.................... use text message spelling, e.g. C for *see*, R for *are*.</li><li>You can use abbreviations such as *asap* (as soon as possible) and emoticons, e.g. ☺</li><li>Use contractions not ⁷...................., e.g. *I'm* not *I am*.</li><li>Include appropriate greeting, e.g. *Hi Jane*, and ⁸...................., e.g. *All the best* (to someone you don't know very well), *Take care*, *See you soon*, *Love* (to a partner, family member or close friend).</li><li>Finish with your ⁹.................... only, e.g. *Lucy*; don't use titles and surnames, e.g. *Mrs Lucy Brown*.</li><li>To a partner, family member or close friend, add one or more x ¹⁰.................... your name, to represent a kiss.</li></ul>	

3 Work with a partner. Make a list of countries in the world that you would like to visit and the things you would like to see in these countries.

E.g. Egypt – The Pyramids

4 Follow the steps to write your own version of the task in exercise 1.

1 Write a plan for your text.
2 Use ideas from exercise 3 for what to say.
3 Use information from exercise 2 about how to write an informal email.
4 Write a first draft and check the word limit.
5 Swap texts with a partner and suggest ways for your partner to improve their text.
6 Listen to what your partner says about how you can improve your text.
7 Write a second draft and give your text to your teacher.
8 Write a final draft. Use the checklist your teacher gives you to improve your text.

Correspondence – formal letters & emails

ISE I Controlled Written exam (approx. 150 words), Portfolio Section 1 (70-80 words)

1 Read the Portfolio task and the letter that a candidate called Esthér writes for the task. What reason does Esthér give for deciding to do an English course in London?

You want to attend a two-week English course at a school in London. Write a letter to the principal explaining why you have decided to attend the course and asking how much it will cost. Tell him about your previous experience of learning English. (ISE I 2010)

Calle Serrano 18, 3B
Los Molinos
28472
Madrid

The Principal
London School of English
12 Queen Street
London

15 April 2011

Dear Sir,

With reference to your English language courses, I am writing to ask for some information.

I have studied English at school in Spain for many years. In the classes, we learn lots of grammar and vocabulary, but we don't practise speaking and listening very much. I am interested in attending a course at your school because I think it will help me improve my speaking and listening skills.

I would like to do a two-week course, at the beginning of July. Can you tell me how much this will cost?

Yours faithfully,

Esthér Garcia Jiminez
Esthér Garcia Jiminez

2 Using Esthér's letter to help you, complete the information about formal emails and letters with words/phrases from the box.

> ask for   contraction   date   don't know   finish   first
> full name   greeting   recipient's address   sender's address

Purpose	• to ¹................... or give information • to give reasons • to request action	
Typical readers	• someone at a business/other organisation; you ²................... this person.	
	Emails	**Letters**
Organisation and layout	• Write on email software and print out. • Date can be in your own language (it is generated automatically). • Complete the subject line (not included in word count). • separate paragraphs for each theme	• ³................... goes at top right-hand side of letter. • ⁴................... goes at top left-hand side of letter. • ⁵................... goes below sender's address.
	• Explain reasons for writing in ⁶................... paragraph • ⁷................... with concluding paragraph.	
Features	• Language style is neutral to formal. • Language structures and functions depend on purpose of email/letter, e.g. connecting clauses using *because* to give reasons. • Use full forms not contractions, e.g. *I am* not *I'm*, but you can use the ⁸................... *don't* instead of *do not*. • Use standard ⁹................... and ending, i.e. Dear Sir/Madam, Yours faithfully; Dear Mrs Green, Yours sincerely. • Finish with your signature and your ¹⁰................... under this	

3 Work with a partner and follow the instructions.

1 Make a list of possible reasons for doing an English course in London.
E.g. *to meet British people*

2 Make notes about your previous experience of learning English.
E.g. *classes every week at a private language school*

4 Follow the steps to write your own answer to the task in exercise 1.

1 Write a plan for your text.

2 Use ideas from exercise 3 for what to say.

3 Use information from exercise 2 about how to write a formal email.

4 Write a first draft and check the word limit.

5 Swap texts with a partner and suggest ways for your partner to improve their text.

6 Listen to what your partner says about how you can improve your text.

7 Write a second draft and give your text to your teacher.

8 Write a final draft. Use the checklist your teacher gives you to improve your text.

writing file

Factual writing – reports

ISE I Controlled Written exam (approx. 150 words), Portfolio Section 2 (110-130 words)

1 Read the Writing task about stress and the report that a candidate called Fabián writes for the task. Do you think Fabián's suggestions for treating stress would work?

Many people today complain that they suffer from stress. Write a report for a fitness group saying what the most common causes and symptoms of stress are, and suggesting what people can do to treat stress. Write around 130 words.

Stress – causes and cures

Stress is a serious condition that can be responsible for a number of mental and physical problems. Below, we will look firstly at possible causes of stress; secondly, at common symptoms of stress; then, finally, at ways of treating stress.

Common causes

- unhappiness in personal and family relationships
- worry about your school or work situation
- worry about money

Symptoms

- feeling tired all the time
- loss of appetite or overeating
- problems concentrating on studying or work

Treatment

- Avoid drinks containing caffeine, which can make some symptoms of stress worse.
- Talking to people about problems can help.
- Doing exercise can make you feel less stressed.

If you try all of the above, but still feel stressed, then it may be a good idea to see a doctor.

2 Using Fabián's report to help you, complete the information about reports with words/phrases from the box.

> 'signposting' back continuous factual going
> group headings specialist suggestions title

Purpose	• to give ¹................... information about something, e.g. a subject, an event, a problem • to make ²................... about what to do, based on the information you have presented
Typical readers	• readers of a ³................... magazine or website, or members of a special interest ⁴................... e.g. school/college magazine or website readers, members of a health and fitness club
Organisation and layout	• Not necessarily organised into paragraphs of ⁵................... text. Instead, you can use bullet points to mark each individual point or sentence. • Use ⁶................... to mark different sections. • Include a ⁷................... that describes the contents of the report. • Start by stating what the report is about and how it is organised, i.e. ⁸................... .
Features	• Language style is neutral to formal. • Usually more objective and factual than articles. • Use words such as below to refer to something you are ⁹................... to say or *above* to refer ¹⁰................... to something you have already said. • If the task involves making a suggestion or recommendation, include expressions for these functions.

3 Work in pairs. Read the writing task about health and fitness and brainstorm ideas for what to include in it.

Many people today do not take enough exercise. Write a report for a health and fitness group saying what you think will happen if this continues, what people need to do to get fit and why it is important to take regular exercise. Write around 130 words. (ISE I 2011)

4 Follow the steps to write your response to the task in exercise 3.

   1 Write a plan for your text.
   2 Use ideas from exercise 3 for what to say.
   3 Use information from exercise 2 about how to write a report.
   4 Write a first draft and check the word limit.
   5 Swap texts with a partner and suggest ways for your partner to improve their text.
   6 Listen to what your partner says about how you can improve your text.
   7 Write a second draft and give your text to your teacher.
   8 Write a final draft. Use the checklist your teacher gives you to improve your text.

writing file

Factual writing – reviews

ISE I Controlled Written exam (approx. 150 words), Portfolio Section 2 (110-130 words)

1 Read the Portfolio task and the review that a candidate called Mario writes for the task. What age group do you think Mario is thinking about in her review?

A new shopping centre has just opened in your area. Write a review for your local paper saying how well the shops and facilities cater for your age group and how popular you think the shopping centre will be. Write around 130 words. (ISE I 2008)

Tilbury Super centre

The new Tilbury Super centre opened for the first time last Saturday. It is open from 10 a.m. to 10 p.m. every day of the year, except 25th December.

This centre has a supermarket, clothes shops, electrical goods stores, mobile phone shops and plenty of cafes and restaurants. The teenage market is well catered for, with two video game stores, three sports shops and a bike shop. There are also a number of clothes shops with prices and styles for the younger end of the market. The cafés and restaurants will appeal to young people, too.

I think that Tilbury has everything to make it very popular with younger people, except there's no public transport to the centre. So, if they're too young to drive, they'll have to ask their parents to give them a lift!

2 Using Mario's review to help you, complete the information about reviews with words/phrases from the box.

> factual   feelings   finish   formal
> informal   performance   personal   start

Purpose	• to give a ¹.................... opinion, and some ².................... information, about a place, a product, a book, a song, or a ³...................., e.g. a concert, a film, a play
Typical readers	• reader of a magazine, newspaper or website • someone who is thinking about going to the place, reading the book, seeing the performance, etc. in the review
Organisation and layout	• Include a title (not part of word count). • Organise text into paragraphs. • ⁴.................... with basic factual information. • Go on to give more details. • Mention good and bad points. • ⁵.................... with your opinion and recommendation to the reader.
Features	• Language style is often neutral to formal, but depends on the readers, e.g. a review of a rock concert for a music magazine will be ⁶...................., a review of a book for a literary magazine more ⁷.................... . • Include language for giving opinions and describing positive and negative ⁸.................... .

3 Work with a partner. Choose a shopping centre in your area and make a list of what you like and don't like about it.

4 Follow the steps to write your own answer to the task in exercise 1.

   1 Write a plan for your text.

   2 Use ideas from exercise 3 for what to say.

   3 Use information from exercise 2 about how to write a review.

   4 Write a first draft and check the word limit.

   5 Swap texts with a partner and suggest ways for your partner to improve their text.

   6 Listen to what your partner says about how you can improve your text.

   7 Write a second draft and give your text to your teacher.

   8 Write a final draft. Use the checklist your teacher gives you to improve your text.

Factual Writing – articles

ISE I Controlled Written exam (approx. 150 words), Portfolio Section 2 (110-130 words)

1 Read the Writing task about individual and team sports and the article that a candidate called Hao writes in response. Does Hao think that individual or team sports are better?

Write an article for a sports club website with the title 'Team sports versus individual sports'. Describe the advantages of both types of sport, then say which you personally think are better. Write around 130 words.

Football or tennis? Basketball or running? Playing on your own or playing with a team?

On the one hand, team sports can be more motivating and they can also help you learn how to work with other people. It's also nice to share the excitement of winning and the disappointment if you lose the game.

On the other hand, individual sports also have advantages. Firstly, it is your decision when to play. Secondly, you're not dependent on other people – winning or losing is your responsibility. Also, if you win, you don't have to share the glory – or the prizes!

However, I don't think it's possible to say whether team sports or individual sports are better. There are advantages to both, but, ultimately, the sport you do has to be one that you enjoy.

writing file

2 Using Hao's article to help you, complete the information about articles with words/phrases from the box.

> *attention   different   information   introducing   neutral   opinion   paragraphs   website*

Purpose	• to give factual ¹................... about something • to discuss and argue a point • to give your ²................... about something
Typical readers	• readers of a magazine, newspaper or ³....................
Organisation and layout	• Organise the text into ⁴................... . • Try to start the article with an interesting statement or question that attracts the reader's ⁵.................... .
Features	• Language style is ⁶................... to formal, depending on readers. • If appropriate, include words and phrases for ⁷................... a point of view and giving a ⁸................... point of view, and adding more points and contrasting points. • Include phrases for giving your opinion, as necessary.

3 Underline words and phrases in the article in exercise 1 that are used for:

- introducing a point of view
- adding more points
- making contrasting points.

4a Read the Writing task about school uniforms.

Write an article for your school website with the title 'School uniform – a good idea?'. Describe the advantages for young people of having and not having school uniform, then say which you personally think is better. Write around 130 words.

b Work in pairs. Make two lists: one of the advantages for young people of having a school uniform; the other of the advantages of not having a school uniform.

5 Follow the steps to write your response to the task in exercise 4.

1 Write a plan for your text.

2 Use ideas from exercise 4 for what to say.

3 Use information from exercise 2 about how to write an article.

4 Use words and phrases that you underlined in exercise 3.

5 Write a first draft and check the word limit.

6 Swap texts with a partner and suggest ways for your partner to improve their text.

7 Listen to what your partner says about how you can improve your text.

8 Write a second draft and give your text to your teacher.

9 Write a final draft. Use the checklist your teacher gives you to improve your text.

Creative writing – a story or description

ISE I Controlled Written exam (approx. 150 words), Portfolio Section 3 (110-130 words)

1 Read the Portfolio task for a story and look at the mind map that a candidate called Hans has prepared and the story he has written based on this mind map.

Write a story for a writing competition about a poor family who won a lot of money on the lottery. Explain how much money they won, what they did with it and how it changed their lives. (ISE I 2010)

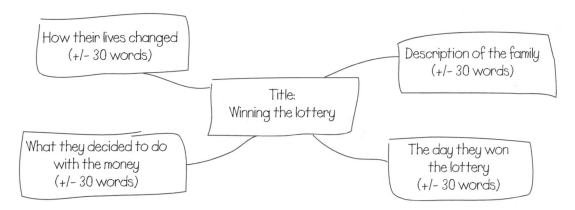

How their lives changed (+/- 30 words)

Description of the family (+/- 30 words)

Title: Winning the lottery

What they decided to do with the money (+/- 30 words)

The day they won the lottery (+/- 30 words)

WINNING THE LOTTERY

Mr and Mrs Perez lived in a small village with their three children. They worked hard but they didn't have much money. Their house was tiny and the children all slept in one room.

One Friday night, as usual, they watched the lottery show on television and – believe it or not – they saw that they were the lucky winners! The prize was 13 million euros!

They talked about how they could spend the money – a big house, a car, a holiday – and the children all made lists of the things they wanted.

A year later they had everything but they were not happy. The children stayed in their separate bedrooms all day playing computer games and nobody went to work. In fact, they were all bored!

2 Now compare the mind map and the story carefully. Note how each box in the mind map leads to one paragraph of the story.

3 Using the mind map, the story and the words below in the box, complete this information about writing stories and descriptions.

amuse *plan* *past* *paragraphs* *punctuation* *adjectives* *style* *title* *like* *familiar* *imagine*

Purpose	• to entertain, 0 ...*amuse*... or interest your readers
	• to describe a place, a person, an object, a situation etc.
	• to tell people about a 1.................. event or series of events
	• to enable your reader to 2.................. something, someone etc.
Typical readers	• a friend or member of your family
	• people 3.................. yourself
	• people who are not 4.................. with the thing, person, event etc. that you are writing about
Organisation and layout	• Organise your writing in 5.................. – one for each idea.
	• Use a mind map to 6.................. your story or description – you can write one paragraph for each box in your mind map.
	• Use lots of describing words such as 7.................. and adverbs.
Features	• You should give your writing a 8.................. (not included in the word count)
	• It can be informal or formal, depending on the reader(s) but most ISE I portfolio tasks need an informal 9.................. .
	• You can use contractions such as *doesn't*, *we'd* etc. if you are writing in an informal style.
	• Language structure and functions may differ but we usually use Past Simple and Past Continuous for a story and Present or Past Simple for a description.
	• Accurate spelling, grammar and 10.................. are expected.

4 Now look at this task for writing a description. Decide who you are going to write about and make a mind map with some ideas to include in your description.

Write a description for a popular magazine of a person you admire a lot. Describe their appearance and personality and explain why you think this person is so special. (ISE I 2007)

5 Follow the steps in the list below to produce your description.

1 Calculate the word limit for each paragraph.

2 Write a first draft and check the number of words.

3 Swap descriptions with a partner and suggest ways for your partner to improve their description.

4 Write a second draft and give your description to your teacher.

5 When you get it back from your teacher, write a final draft. Use the checklist your teacher gives you to improve your description.

Creative writing – an entry in a diary

ISE I Controlled Written exam (approx. 150 words), Portfolio Section 3 (110-130 words)

1 Read the Portfolio task and look at the mind map that a candidate has prepared and the diary entry she has written based on this mind map.

Write the diary of a pop star on the day when he/she performed his/her first concert. (ISE I 2007)

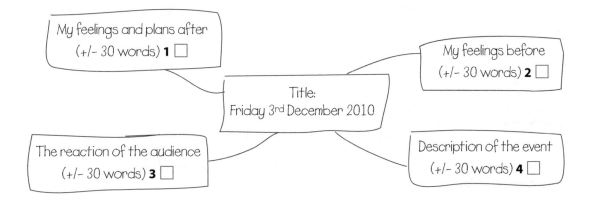

My feelings and plans after (+/– 30 words) **1** ☐

My feelings before (+/– 30 words) **2** ☐

Title:
Friday 3rd December 2010

The reaction of the audience (+/– 30 words) **3** ☐

Description of the event (+/– 30 words) **4** ☐

Saturday 4th December, 2010

A My first concert last night!!! So nervous! I've really never felt so nervous before in my life! Could hear the audience from the dressing room and that made me even more scared!

B I was first on the stage and I sang two songs. I'd rehearsed and rehearsed and I didn't forget any of the words. Before I knew it, it was finished and I was back in the dressing room.

C The audience didn't exactly go wild but they didn't walk out, either! In fact, to be honest, some of them were shouting for more.

D They were still clapping and whistling as I left the stage. Felt absolutely great – dream come true! Next Friday, same place, same time, different songs! Must remember to invite Peter!

2 Now compare the mind map and the diary carefully. Match the paragraphs of the diary entry (1-4) to the different boxes on the mind map.

3 Using the diary entry and the information below in the box, complete the empty column with a tick (✓) if you can find that feature in the diary entry. The first one has been done for you.

Purpose	• to make a record of events • to make a record of thoughts and feelings	✓
Typical readers	• probably only yourself	
Organisation and layout	• A diary entry may be written in separate paragraphs or as a single paragraph.	
Features	• There is not normally a title for a diary entry. • Instead of a title there will be a date (not included in the word count) • The language is very informal, for example, we often miss out pronouns and articles. • Punctuation can also be very informal, for example: we may use two or three exclamation or question marks we may use dashes (-) instead of commas or full stops	

4 Find these phrases in the example text and put back the words that would be there if it was written in a more formal style.

My first concert last night!	→	0 It was my first concert last night!
So nervous!	→	1
Could hear the audience	→	2
Felt absolutely great	→	3
dream come true	→	4
Must remember…	→	5

5a Here is another task for writing a diary entry. Work with a partner to write a list of typical resolutions that people make at the start of a new year.

Write your diary entry for 1st January. Say what different things you are planning to do in the coming year and explain how these New Year's resolutions will improve your life. (ISE I 2009)

b Follow the steps in the list below to produce your text.

1 Make a mind map for your diary – put the date in the centre.
2 Calculate the word limit for each paragraph.
3 Write a first draft and check the number of words.
4 Read through your draft – has it got some of the features from exercise 3?
5 Swap diaries with a partner and suggest ways for your partner to improve their diary entry.
6 Write a second draft and give your diary entry to your teacher.
7 When you get it back from your teacher, write a final draft. Use the checklist your teacher gives you to improve your diary entry.

Controlled Written exam – Reading into Writing task

45 minutes (approx. 150 words)

> The Reading into Writing task tests your ability to transfer information from a reading text into a piece of your own writing. You must take ideas from the reading text, but you **must not** copy whole phrases or sentences.

1a Read the task and text 'Walks in London'.

You and a friend are planning a trip to England and want to go for a walk in London. Read the text below and then, in your own words, write a letter (approximately 150 words) to your friend explaining:

*i) which walk you think will be the most suitable for you and your friend **and***

ii) why the other two walks do not interest you. (ISE I 2009)

Walks in London

Take a walk around London and discover what the capital city has to offer. There's lots to explore and some great rivers, parks and attractions!

River walk — 7 kilometres
This walk will take you along the River Thames. You will pass a number of landmarks, including the London Eye and the Tate Modern art museum. You will also see eight of London's many bridges. If you do the walk on a Thursday or Friday, you can buy some traditional English food at Borough food market.

Park walk — 8 kilometres
Escape the city and discover London's largest park — Richmond Park. This relaxing walk starts at the Gate Café and it will take you around the park. With its woodlands, flower gardens and famous deer park, it's one of London's most beautiful treasures. Bring a picnic and really enjoy the beauty of the park.

City walk — 5 kilometres
See some of the oldest parts of London including the Roman wall and the places where the Great Fire of London started and ended in 1666. Tourist attractions include the Bank of England, the Museum of London and the Tower of London. A weekend is probably the best time to do this walk, as there will be less traffic and people.

b Now put the paragraphs (A-C) of Li's answer to the task in the correct order.

Dear Jimmy,
How are you?
A ☐ The other walks don't look as interesting and the Park walk isn't even in Central London. The City walk only includes one small area of London and it may be busy because we'll do our walk on a Thursday.
B ☐ I'm writing about our trip to London next week. I've done some research into walks that we can do. In particular, I've looked at three walks from a website about London.
C ☐ I've chosen the River walk. It's 7 kilometres – not too long and not too short. It will give us lots of opportunities to see famous landmarks, like the London Eye, and we'll have really good views of the River Thames because the walk includes 8 bridges. We can even do some shopping for traditional food at a market!
I hope you agree with my choice. See you next week,
Love,
Li x

2a Work with a partner. Choose one of the other two walks and write three reasons why you chose it.

b Now write three reasons why you don't want to do the other walks.

3 Write your answer to the task in exercise 1. Include the reasons you gave in exercise 2.

appendix 1 Extra material

Unit 3, page 26, exercise 3a

Film quiz answers:

1A **2**A **3**B **4**C **5**C **6**B **7**C **8**A

Unit 5, page 44, exercise 5b

The following graphs show the percentage of income that people in different countries spend on four different things: housing, food & drink, health and education.

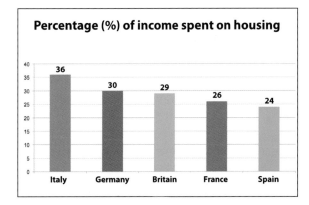

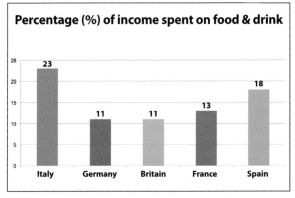

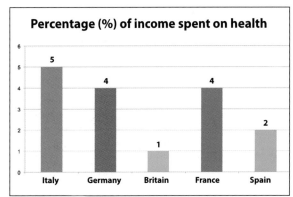

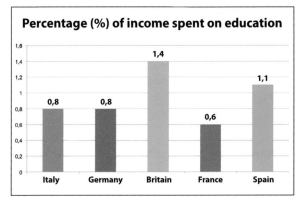

Unit 7, page 62, exercise 8b

1 Miami, USA   **2** Singapore   **3** Britain   **4** Britain   **5** France   **6** Florida, USA   **7** Vermont, USA
8 Britain   **9** Athens, Greece   **10** Arkansas, USA   **11** Britain

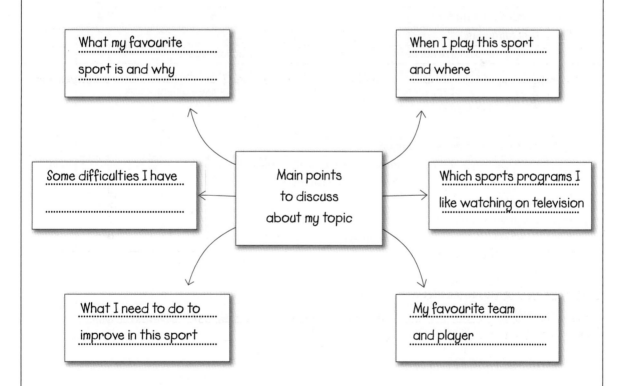

**Graded Examinations in Spoken English
Elementary Topic form – Grade 6**

Name: ....

Grade 6   Registration no: ....

Centre: ....   Session: ....

Centre no: ....   Examination date: ....

Title of topic: ..... My favourite sport ....

What my favourite sport is and why	When I play this sport and where
Some difficulties I have	Main points to discuss about my topic	Which sports programs I like watching on television
What I need to do to improve in this sport	My favourite team and player

The information on this form must be presented to the examiner during the exmination.

Note: This topic form has been created as an example. See the Trinity College syllabus for the original form.

Student Portfolio feedback form

Candidate name: .... ISE 0 ☐ ISE I ☐ ISE II ☐ ISE III ☐ ISE IV ☐

Teacher name: .... Date: ....

Task section: .... Centre (name or number): ....

Teachers are strongly recommended to give candidates feedback in the preparation of their portfolios.

Teachers should complete just one copy of this sheet for each task presented by the candidate. It should be completed by ticking appropriate items in the right-hand column. This sheet must be the only form of feedback between teacher and candidate. When completed, this form should be handed to the candidate.

The candidate must ensure that it is attached to the final version and included in the portfolio.

Advice to the student	✓
Task fulfilment	
Parts of the task have not been completed — look at the instructions again	
The task does not meet the requirements set — look at the instructions again	
This work does not appear to be entirely your own — you must choose a different task	
Your work contains some irrelevant details and/or repetition	
You should add some more ideas	
You should give more description	
The format, style and/or register are not appropriate to the task	
The task is too long/short — check the word length range	
Organisation	
Your presentation and/or layout need to be improved	
You should check and improve paragraphing	
You need to add an introduction	
You need to add a conclusion	
You need to rewrite the task with more legible handwriting or word-process your work	
Grammar	
You need to check and improve the grammar of your work	
You should use a greater range of grammatical structures	
You need to check your word order	
Vocabulary	
You should use a greater range of vocabulary	
You need to check you are using the correct words	
Spelling/Punctuation	
You should check the spellings of words in your work	
You should check and improve the punctuation in your work	

Note: This form has been created as an example. See the Trinity College syllabus for the original form.

1 How is my interview graded?

Pass grades: **A** – Distinction, **B** – Merit, **C** – Pass   Fail grade: **D**

2 How does the examiner assess my interview?

For **Grades 5** and **6** and **ISE I** you must fulfil the task in each phase of the interview – the Topic and Conversation. (See Trinity Syllabus for communicative skills, grammatical, lexical, and phonological items for each level.) In addition she/he will look at fluency and promptness of response for the level.

3 How is my Portfolio and Controlled Written exam work in ISE I graded?

A – Excellent, **B** – Good, **C** – Satisfactory, **D** – Almost satisfactory, **E** – Not satisfactory

4 What is the examiner looking for in my Portfolio and Controlled Written exam tasks?

You must fulfil the tasks by using a range of appropriate vocabulary and grammar used accurately. Your writing must be organised coherently, with accurate spelling and punctuation.

5 How are my marks calculated?

The final marks are calculated and then confirmed in London, see below for weighting.

		Task within component	Component within the exam
ISE I Controlled Written exam	Task 1 Task 2	50% 50%	30%
ISE I Portfolio	Correspondence task	20%	20%
	Factual writing task	40%	
	Creative/descriptive writing	40%	
ISE I Interview	Topic	50%	50%
	Discussion of Portfolio and conversation	50%	
Grades 5 and 6	Topic	50%	100%
	Conversation	50%	

6 What percentage do I need to get in total to pass the exam? And what about passing with Merit or Distinction?

Pass – 65%, Merit – 75%, Distinction – 85%

7 What happens if I don't get a pass grade in one part of the exam?

In **Grades 5 and 6**, you will be able to use look-up tables to convert grades to Pass/Fail.

In **ISE I**, to get an overall pass grade, you must get a pass in both parts of the exam.

8 If I get a fail result, will the examiner tell me why?

Yes. The report indicates areas for improvement under these headings: communicative skills, grammar, lexis and phonology.

Internet: www.blackcat-cideb.com
email: info@blackcat-cideb.com

Editors: Joanna Burgess, Maria Grazia Donati
Book and cover design: Maura Santini
Page layout: Annalisa Possenti
Illustrations: Giovanni Da Re
Design coordinator: Simona Corniola
Picture research: Alice Graziotin

Art Director: Nadia Maestri

Picture Credits
t: top   c: centre   b: bottom   r: right   l: left
Cideb Archive; Getty Images: 12c, b; David Poblador i Garcia/CC 3.0: 21t; Kevin Mazur/EM/Getty Images: 25l; Michael Ochs Archives/Getty Images: 25b; Kevin Mazur/Getty Images: 29.

Printed in Italy by Stamperia Artistica Nazionale, Trofarello, Turin

Reprint			V	VI
Year	2013	2014	2015	2016